∼ *Inner Visions* ∼

Gemstone (Wilfried Satty)

Inner Visions

Explorations in magical consciousness

Nevill Drury

Routledge & Kegan Paul
London, Boston and Henley

First published in 1979
by Routledge & Kegan Paul Ltd
39 Store Street, London WC1E 7DD,
Broadway House, Newtown Road,
Henley-on-Thames, Oxon RG9 1EN and
9 Park Street, Boston, Mass. 02108, USA
Set in 10 on 13pt Palatino
and printed in Great Britain by
Lowe & Brydone Printers Ltd,
Thetford, Norfolk
Plates printed by
The Scolar Press Ltd
Ilkley, West Yorkshire
©Nevill Drury 1979

British Library Cataloguing in Publication Data

Drury, Nevill
Inner visions.
1. Magic – Psychological aspects
I. Title
133.4   BF1611   79-40254

ISBN 0 7100 0257 2
ISBN 0 7100 0184 3 Pbk

The tinted air glowed before me with intelligible significance like a face, a voice. The visible world became like a tapestry blown and stirred by winds behind it . . . .
Every form on that tapestry appeared to be the work of gods.

A. E. The Candle of Vision

Contents

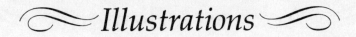Illustrations

Acknowledgments

The author and publishers are grateful to the following for permission to reproduce illustrations: Ernst Fuchs for *Paradiesbaum* and the detail from *Kampf der vervandelten Gotter*; Wilfried Satty for *Gemstone, Child and Signs in the Sky*, *The Haunted Palace* and *The Virgin Land*; Société de la Propriété Artistique et des Dessins et Modèles for *Birth of the Galaxy* by Max Ernst, *Sleeping Venus* by Paul Delvaux and *Beliar* by Wilfredo Lam, © by S.P.A.D.E.M. Paris, 1978; Association pour la Diffusion des Arts Graphiques et Plastiques for *Santiago El Grande* by Salvador Dali and *The Musings of a Solitary Walker* by René Magritte © by A.D.A.G.P. Paris, 1978; Kenneth Grant, author of *Images and Oracles of Austin Osman Spare*, for *Farewell to Synthesis* by Austin Osman Spare; Roger Dean for *Relayer* and *Chartbusters* (vol. 6) © Roger Dean from the book of his work *Views* published by Dragon's Dream Ltd; Patrick Woodroffe for *The Bull and the Spear*; H. R. Giger and Sphinx Verlag for *The Spell*, parts I and II © H. R. Giger, from H. R. Giger's *Necronomicon* © 1977 Sphinx Verlag Basel; Abdul Mati Klarwein for *What am I doing with my Life?*; Johfra Bosschart for the central panel of *Unio Mystica, Libra* and *Gemini*; Diana Vandenberg for *Rex et Regina II*; Rosaleen Norton for *Individuation* and *Panic*; and Tom Akawie of Berkeley, California for *Cloud Mirror*.

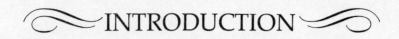

Counter-culture, magic and the new consciousness

During a recent interview historian Theodore Roszak commented on the revival of occult and metaphysical beliefs in modern Western society — a somewhat surprising feature of an era which is host to a rapidly spawning technology. The beginnings of our culture, he noted, were characterized by a sense of magic and mystery. He went on to say:[1]

> Some people say that our culture has been a development from subjectivity to objectivity — from fantasy to reality — and that is the way things should go. But I see it in a different way. I believe that transition involved a certain loss in our culture and what people are doing on the Aquarian frontier is trying to bring myth, magic and mystery back into our lives.

It is clear that the environment of pre-rational man was essentially an unfathomable and awe-inspiring locale in which superior forces and energies were thought to be at work, and even up until the industrial period institutionalized religion has endeavoured to define ultimate causes and effects. Traditionally man has designated these levels of causality as gods and spirits, aligning them either for or against man and regarding them as being in need of placation, supplication and reverent worship. Magic, whether by ritual or trance, fetish or incantation, is a technique of having rapport with the gods — the ultimate reality associated with one's culture—and a means of defining one's own identity within the matrix of existence. Now, according to Roszak, we have seen a period of transition with the evolution of the scientific world-view. Over centuries, and with haste since the growth of rational thought, we have seen myth transformed into history, magic into reason, and mystery (fear and awe for the world) into technology and the attempted domination of the earth's resources. Roszak succinctly describes this process as one which turns its back on the 'visionary sources of our culture', the coming of a world-view which, for the first

1

time lays prime emphasis on technological achievement ahead of the cosmological explanation of reality, and which focuses existentially on the nature of man devoid of any suggestion of mystical or magical origins.

Despite the growth of a vastly complex mechanistic environment in our urban sprawl, certain philosophies of reaction have emerged and some of these may be grouped together in terms of what has been called the 'consciousness movement'. This movement is not a movement in the sense of a brigade or even a single line of thought, but constitutes a body of views and attitudes which challenges the prevailing scientific world-view, not so much in terms of its value as a means of ordering knowledge and factual data, but in terms of its pre-eminence as a belief system. Various commentators have raised the question of the actual level of consciousness of our scientists. They have queried their grasp of issues such as uranium mining and storage of nuclear waste, which affect man and his interaction with the environment, and the directions and consequences for future generations in our society. The consciousness movement is composed of many voices from many disciplines, each reacting against 'scientism' in his particular domain. Included are ecologists like William Irwin Thompson, founder of the Lindisfarne community on Long Island. Also parapsychologists and mind researchers like Jean Houston and Robert Masters, Charles Tart, John Lilly, Andrew Weil and Montague Ullman, who continue to provide data pertaining to a view of man which transcends the limited notion of a stimulus and response organism whose aesthetic and ethical values may be identified with a chemical DNA pattern or an electrical charge in the brain. We also find in this consciousness development, a new consideration for the study of mythology as a metaphorical expression of different features of the temperament of man.

Of course, a whole gamut of religious practices, cults and groups has come along in the train of this renewed mystical inclination. There are Hare Krishnas, Children of God, Scientologists, followers of the Korean evangelist Sun Moon, spokesmen for the Divine Light Mission of Guru Maharaj Ji, astrologers, cosmologers, numerologists, palm readers, visionaries and frauds – all in dazzling array.

Readers of Alvin Toffler's *Future Shock* could be forgiven for supposing that these multifarious cults are a symptom of the pressure of technological change and that they represent signs of weakness among those who cannot sustain the pace, producing instead a huddling in groups, a turning away from the external world to the security of the ashram, the meditation centre, the small circle of known friends. There is of course an element of truth in this, but it seems to me mistaken to leave it at that. If the ashrams and transcendental meditation centres, and the corresponding growth of the guru circuit and all manner of what the Anglican church recently termed 'occultish practices'[2] *are* with us, it is surely necessary to ask what value or alternative reality they propose, and ask why it is that they have appeared during this period of social history.

There seem to be common features underlying this vast assortment of groupings and practices – features which align bodies like Friends of the Earth with a group like the Ananda Marga, one an ecological movement, the other a Tantric sect. Both are concerned with the sanctity of the environment, both are outraged at the violation of natural resources. The consciousness movement embraces both the ecological issues and also the terrain of man's mind, a base assumption being that man acts according to his perceptions, his world-view and his belief systems. If his world-view is unenlightened his acts will similarly be so. If his range of causality is defined as occurring within certain parameters of 'reality', his actions, beliefs and social structure will mirror that distinction.

The consciousness movement seems to be asking collectively: what is the fullest span of perception accessible to man; what is his most deeply felt sense of reality and of what does it consist? How should man act?

The feeling that behaviour is a symptom of that grey area called 'consciousness' has led many scientifically trained psychologists, social anthropologists and writers into what would normally be regarded as highly intangible and subjective areas.

Professor Charles Tart, a clinical psychologist at the University of California, Davis, undertook early research into behaviour patterns associated with marijuana and alcohol, but it is significant that his more recent work, as exemplified by *Transpersonal Psychologies*, has gravitated squarely towards the study of altered states of consciousness and the usefulness of certain belief systems like Zen, Hinduism and Sufism as a means of comprehending inner regions of the psyche. He has also undertaken experiments on subjects who under hypnosis mutually deepened each other's state of trance – with surprising results. The subjects found themselves travelling through symbolic locales – tunnels opening out into regions filled with a mystical light – and undergoing experiences rather like rites of passage or initiation. The subjects seem to have been able to communicate both non-verbally and telepathically in a way which excluded Tart himself from any longer fully controlling all the aspects precipitated by the experiment. Meanwhile the subjects came to look upon their deep trance experiences as profoundly real, and very much as symptomatic of a viable alternative reality.[3]

Tart recently proposed what could prove in time to be an extremely valuable concept—that we should identify what he calls 'state-specific sciences'. As a clinical analyst Tart has not turned his back on the need for rigorous scientific investigation but has merely pointed out that science is normally conducted within the precincts of what has come to be known as the 'consensus reality' – the reality out there that we all agree upon as the basis for communication, language and normal daily activity. The fact arises however that we now have knowledge of *altered* states of consciousness – non-consensus states where several of the rules of normal perception and causality appear not to apply.

For example, numerous studies have been made of out-of-the-body-experiences by scientific observers such as Tart himself, Karlis Osis, Celia Green, Harold Puthoff, Russell Targ, Jean Houston and Stanley Krippner. During an out-of-the-body-experience the subject may experience the sensation of observing his own body in trance or at rest while his faculties of perception are to all extents and purposes operating from another point in space, some distance removed. The subject finds himself able to move at will, to pass through physical objects like walls and ceilings and yet to observe phenomena in the consensus reality as if from a different frame of reference. Our subject may also find himself encountering subconscious images, either pertaining to his own personal identity or arising from a deep mythological source, as if they were equally real. Sounds could perhaps acquire colours, and colours scents, as if a whole new range of perceptive sensitivity had been opened up.

The parapsychologists who are foremost in the consciousness investigation have not been content with sweeping these experiences away by labelling them as psychotic or schizoid but have instead undertaken experiments to attempt to identify basic common denominators in these areas of mind–body research.

For example, Dr Joseph Kamiya of the Langley Porter Institute in San Francisco and Drs Elmer and Alyce Green of the Menninger Institute in Kansas, have undertaken laboratory tests on the brain wave patterns of meditative subjects who are able to alter their range of consciousness by will and in so doing alter the rate of heart pulsation, blood flow and several of the body's automatic functions. These techniques have given rise to the biofeedback approach of learning to maintain the deep relaxation states characterized by alpha brain wave activity.

The analysis in these areas has been thorough but the experiences of the subjects undergoing testing has sometimes pointed to new factors of causality, apparently beyond the domain of current scientific models. Charles Tart's suggestion of state-specific sciences, meanwhile, posits the notion that data arrived at as the result of the systematic personal exploration of inner states and alternative realities is equally valuable to that derived from the laboratory, *but each pertains to a certain set of circumstances*. Mystical experiences, for example, have both a physiological and also an aesthetic dimension.

Consequently, much of the most significant material which is emerging from the new consciousness movement has to do with inner states of mind, with creative and ethical faculties, and that old utopian concept of the potential of man.

While the early phase of the counter-culture perhaps had a preponderance of interests in *effects* – particularly of drugs like LSD, mescalin, DMT, and marijuana – the present development seems to me to be both more sober and less overtly spectacular, but also more penetrating. Among the 'new consciousness' exponents of the 1970s we find John Lilly undertaking his inner voyages in the disciplined tranquillity of a sensory deprivation tank in Maryland, and documenting his experiences in terms of mathematical vibrationary levels like +3, +6, +48 and so on. His more recent work, particularly that in *Simulations of God* (a book which might eventually prove more significant than *Centre of the Cyclone*), begins to analyse the very nature of belief systems. Lilly asks about the range of consciousness available through means of a set of religious beliefs and ideas – are they liberating or constricting? He notes that a crucial aim is to identify the limits of one's beliefs and then transcend them, a truly open-ended cosmology.

This is very much a step forward since the counter-culture's mystical contingent is cluttered with groups and sects embracing both Eastern and Western beliefs, and Lilly's proposal is to move beyond this sectarianism into a consideration of the area of inner consciousness which actually gives rise to a belief system and leads us to prefer one dogma to another.

5

The movement towards a type of universalism is also found in the work of Robert Masters and Jean Houston, directors of the Foundation for Mind Research, New York, who evolved a series of 'mind games'. These games are activities in which subjects, usually in a group, develop their sensory imagination to the extent that they begin to feel, taste and perceive more acutely. The more advanced games take the subjects into deep trance states by means of having them imagine themselves undertaking what in another culture would be regarded as a mythological journey—down into the earth, across inner space oceans and into magical situations involving transformation. Masters and Houston are using these techniques to plumb the creative imagination. In shamanistic cultures, such as those found in Siberia and Central America, the ecstatic would journey in trance to the land of the ancestors. Perhaps he would be shown sacred mysteries pertaining to the origin of his culture or undergo rituals of rebirth such as being torn to pieces and then restructured by the gods. In such an instance the shaman would return to his waking consciousness as a man of knowledge, an intermediary with the gods and interpreter of the ancestral images of his culture.

If it is true, as Roszak says, that we have lost touch with this sense of mystery in our identity and being, there are clear indications that the new consciousness development is attempting to counter-balance the mechanistic world-view of man.

This brings me to the subject of the present book. There are many obvious signs in Western society of renewed fascination with occult and esoteric concepts, both as shown in the proliferation of interest in yoga, Tarot, astrology and suchlike, and also in terms of an apparent reduction in public cynicism about these matters. Findhorn and Cleve Backster have, in a sense, legitimized the rather extraordinary notion that one should communicate with the plant kingdom; Kirlian photography with its spectacular documentation of energy discharge around living organisms begins to provide a plausible explanation of what were previously termed 'auras and emanations'. Western medicine finds itself obliged to examine the Eastern fusion of mysticism and acupuncture techniques. And, as mentioned previously, several parapsychologists are beginning to relate the study of altered states of consciousness to mind–body mental disciplines like yogic meditation which can produce those states of mind.

In *Inner Visions* my aim is to describe the modern magical world-view in terms of its relevance to the consciousness movement, and also to examine the relationship of magic to the creative powers of the mind. We have here a system of exploring the images of the psyche, a method for identifying the role of archetypes or motifs which find their way especially into art, literature and music. Certain schools of modern art have stressed the value of meditation, trance and other 'altered' states of mind – the symbolists just prior to the turn of the century, the surrealists, and more recently the fantastic realists, whose influence has been felt in the contemporary aftermath of the psychedelic period. It is also significant that the era 1890-1920 which produced the high point of fantasy book illustration – Edmund Dulac, Arthur Rackham, Harry Clarke, Alastair and Sidney Sime and company – also produced the concentrated magical endeavours found in the Hermetic Order of the Golden Dawn and its offshoots. And we find comparable parallels today. Alongside the Tarot cards and reprinted occult literature by writers like S. L. Mathers, A. E. Waite and Aleister Crowley we find Arthur Rackham and Edmund Dulac reprinted in true media fashion, not only in books but on posters, T shirts and greeting cards as very much a facet of the 1970s inclination. Contemporary graphic art also mirrors these tendencies, and the influence of Dali and Magritte of the surrealist school, as well as Rackham and his peers, is quite apparent. However, the graphic art which embellishes album covers and posters, for example, has often tended to reinterpret the nature of the earlier period so that Roger Dean, whose work owes quite a debt to Rackham, also presents a science-fiction image, in reflecting the contemporary consciousness. Dean's *Views* – a remarkable collection of album cover designs – was the most unlikely number one bestseller in Britain in 1976-7 for those who were not expecting it. But it is also interesting to consider the relationship of the fantasy art on record sleeves to the electronic inner-space music which it often represents. As I hope to demonstrate, these forms of modern music represent one facet of the contemporary reaction against scientism and the search for what Roszak has termed the visionary sources of our culture.

In structuring this book I deal first with the nature of the Western magical world-view and its language of symbols, and later with the way in which these symbols and motifs have re-emerged particularly in the art and music of the 1970s. It seems to me that the atavistic stirring of a magical consciousness has wider ramifications than might have been expected.

It should be emphasized that the contemporary search for a relevant mythology is not a symptom of escapism so much as a quest for identity. If *Inner Visions* does appear to draw on disparate sources, a closer examination of the styles of art, music and magical practices considered will show that these in fact mirror each other. The surrealist approach of the 1920s onwards was a philosophy which demanded the expansion of reality, not a retreat from it, and a similar outlook today prevails in parapsychology and the new consciousness movement. It would be a mistake, for example, to see the new direction as anti-scientific. Researchers like Charles Tart and John Lilly may be more appropriately described as trans-scientific. They have come from a background of rigorous scientific training but are now seeking to expand the frameworks of scientific inquiry.

It is my belief that magic and mythology have a prime place in this new venture inwards. As I have noted, mythology has shown its face in the current revival of fantasy literature, in electronic rock music, and the archetypal roles adopted by its proponents. Even in popular comics, we find such heroes as the Mighty Thor and Captain Marvell! The works of Carlos Castaneda have had their effect not so much because of the transient psychedelic revelations which they include but because they delineate an alternative world-view, a new explanation of causality.

Similarly the new forms of art which I discuss represent a super-natural *realism* and in true surrealist fashion extend reality rather than deny it.

As I hope to show, the consciousness framework of the Tree of Life adopted by the Golden Dawn magicians contemporaneously with the birth of modern psychoanalysis, provides a meaningful system for inquiring into the creative imagination. It correlates mythologies, provides us with metaphorical programmes of belief and contains all the themes of spiritual transformation found in mystical and shamanistic practices elsewhere. It is hardly surprising that psychologists in investigating the deep strata of human consciousness should now find themselves turning to esoteric sources.

In the same way that Jung often claimed that his theory of the archetypes of the collective unconscious was based on a study of a vast number of subjects and case histories, the Golden Dawn was also systematic in its approach. The magical practitioners carefully recorded details of their visionary experiences and initiation — recognition of a specific inner reality depended on the magician accurately describing the symbolic states he or she had entered. A notion of the 'purity' of the mythological experience developed and these sets of symbols gradually enlarged into a series of 'correspondences' – an accumulation of the interrelated mythological imagery which would be observed at certain points upon the meditative Tree of Life.

The most persuasive voice in the Golden Dawn, MacGregor Mathers, took the view, and not without justification, that Westerners are an end product of many centuries of a rich and varied culture, and that its mythology reflected its values and inner modes of consciousness.

In *Inner Visions* my aim is to integrate some of the varied threads which constitute the fabric of the new inquiry. And in the magical and surreal approaches especially, which are now re-emerging in a myriad of shapes and forms, we have a profoundly invigorating and inspiring attitude to man and the cosmos.

The relevance of the contemporary magical revival clearly lies in its inclination towards discovering the primal impulses of the Western creative imagination. If Roszak is right, our present mood is one of re-establishing the mythology of our own being, and with it reaffirming our position in a world from which we have begun to feel alienated.

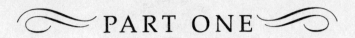

PART ONE

Magic and cosmos

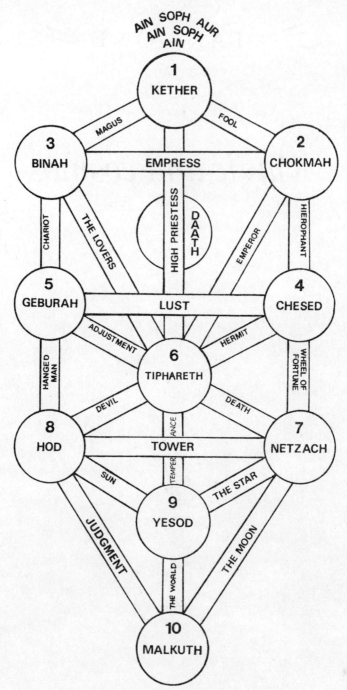

Figure 1 Tree of Life showing Tarot paths

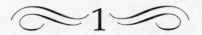

1

The magical universe

The English artist and occultist Austin Spare once wrote that the aim of magic was to steal the fire of heaven, and a quite crucial issue is contained in this statement. The magician, unlike the mystic or religious devotee, believes that he has within his scope and potential, the ability to alter his consciousness magically at will – that the gods will respond to him if he undergoes certain ritual activities. It may be that he dresses ceremonially to conjure their energy by capturing their likeness. Perhaps he utters sacred god names like those found in the Qabalah and certain Gnostic formulations, holding to the view that the name actually embodies the essence of the god, and that by uttering the sacred vibration, he is not only tuning into the wavelength of the God-level, but attaining mastery of it.

The idea of *will* – the sense of being able consciously to bring about a causal effect – is vital to the magical attitude. We find it in the account of Carlos Castaneda, where the magical apprentice has to eat the sacramental drug, whirl the spirit catcher near the sacred water hole and concentrate on the 'spaces' within sounds in order to will the ally to appear.[1] We find it in the magic of Aleister Crowley and the Golden Dawn system in general, where the will enables the magus to rise through the planes of inner space, through the symbolic, mythological energy states of the Tree of Life, and eventually have rapport with the *Higher Self* – anthropomorphized in Crowley's writings as the Holy Guardian Angel.

All of this is quite foreign to most religious systems; prayer and supplication, the offering of thanks to a Saviour god, and ritual activity in a Mass or church service or other worshipful activities, are in no way intended to *capture* the God. Quite the reverse in fact . . . religious devotion is an attitude of mind in which one humbly submits oneself before God in the hope that He will bestow grace and salvation. There is no act of aggression here – no stealing the fire from heaven. One waits, passively, until it is given.

The magical attitude is clearly more active and also more arrogant. The magician is at the centre of his own particular universe. With his sacred formulae, ritual invocations and concentrated will-power, he can bring certain forces to bear. Our first distinction is, then, that the magician believes he can *will* to effect.

The arrogance and even 'primitivism' of this approach has to some extent been made more legitimate by the ascendancy of existential philosophy. It has been common for recent interpreters of the magical tradition to regard the gods of High Magic as emanations and symbols of the creative imagination, forces of the transcendent psyche. Israel Regardie has employed Jungian frameworks of archetypes and energy sources to explain for his contemporary audience what is meant by invoking a God. It is none other than a ritual means of channelling the consciousness into areas described by Jung as the Collective Unconscious, the universal area of the psyche normally inaccessible to man in his everyday activities.

Colin Wilson has similarly related his long involvement with the European existential tradition to a study of modern Western magic, in order to show that such a system of approach offers both a transcendental and an optimistic goal . . . that man *can* overcome his sensory isolation by in fact gauging more universal modes of consciousness and being.

It is only fair to point out however that some occultists view the pantheon of gods as existing in their own right – of being outside the psyche of man – as entities belonging intrinsically to another plane of creation. Magic becomes a means of communication. The gods give knowledge of these esoteric planes to the inquiring magician and allow him to grow in awareness, but they themselves have an identity outside the magician's mind and will. Two examples of magical systems which will be considered, those of the German occultist Franz Bardon, and the Australian witch Rosaleen Norton, both hold this viewpoint.

Magicians irrespective of their cultural milieu do tend to share one feature in common and that is the notion of a hierarchy of supernatural beings with whom they interrelate. In fact remarkably few magical or religious systems are without hierarchy – Zen Buddhism with its 'instant leap into Sartori' being a major example.

If contemporary Western magic has had its roots in Gnosticism, Alchemy, Rosicrucianism and a number of 'pagan' mythologies (the Hellenistic, ancient Egyptian and Celtic systems in particular, all of which exhibit polytheistic features), equivalent hierarchical notions nevertheless present themselves in monotheistic Christianity.

St Thomas Aquinas and other medieval Christian thinkers proposed a hierarchy of angelic beings which reflected different aspects of God's acts in the world. The Seraphim, Cherubim and Thrones were beings related to God Himself—the Father, Son and Holy Ghost; Dominations, Virtues and Powers, related to Universal Creation, and Principalities, Archangels and Angels to individual beings or objects in the world.

Each of these nine orders of Heavenly beings revolved in choirs around God, the Seraphim being closest to God and the Angels furthest removed. The total Heavenly hierarchy thus consisted of God the Father, Son and Holy Ghost, the Virgin Mary, myriads of angels on nine planes, and the order of Saints.[2]

In magic, similarly, the sense of hierarchy is paramount. The medieval *Lesser Key of Solomon* or *Goetia*, which hovers in polarity between black and white magic, contains conjurations to seventy-two devils and also the angels of the hours of day and night, and the signs of the Zodiac. For example, Samael, angelic ruler of the First Hour, is said to have 444 spirits serving under him, and Anael, ruler of the Second Hour has 110. All of this made for most complex and numerous divisions of the supernatural battery of forces encompassing the earth!

Our emphasis in this book is on the modern day, rather than on medieval forms of magical thought, but it is interesting that as recently as 1976, the ceremonial diary of a practitioner of medieval occultism, was published. Georges Chevalier provides in his book *The Sacred Magician* a day-by-day account of his emotional and spiritual reactions in working the lengthy ritual of Abra-Melin the Mage. The actual magical formulation dates from the fifteenth century and takes six months of ritual activity in isolation before the magician is granted communication with his 'Holy Guardian Angel'.

Chevalier's account in many ways is unsatisfactory as a record of magical procedure since it is particularly subjective in style and stresses generalized feelings ('The atmosphere is very difficult around me. Obstacles are being thrown up and I am clumsily stumbling down the path . . .'), rather than a procession of archetypes or magical visions. Chevalier also indicates in his account that he read works such as the Theosophical writings of Alice Bailey and *The Hundred Thousand Songs of Milarepa* during his retreat, thus invalidating to some extent any claim that his results were purely a result of the Abra-Melin method and not produced by meditation on Eastern themes.

However, to attempt a rigorous magical ceremony over such a span of time while remaining in a twentieth century urban context is worthy of note. Interestingly, Chevalier acknowledges a profound sense of spiritual hierarchy. Near the end of his account, at the stage where he has come to identify the regenerative force of his Higher Self, he writes: 'all my communication with the Angels and spirits – with the members of the sub or super-human Hierarchies, – is done on [a] high intuitive level . . . .'[3]

Later, having followed the instructions of Abra-Melin which demand that the magician invoke the eight sub-princes and the four spirits of evil, in order to gain mastery over them, Chevalier notes: 'As one progresses along the Path, there are certain "tests and tribulations" . . . a complete trust in God and the Hierarchy will see one through everything.'[4]

One of the most remarkable magical visions of the present century and certainly the most impressive outside the Golden Dawn tradition is that of Franz Bardon. Bardon, who died in July 1958 in Germany, was known to his Western occult audience through his writings, rather than as a magical personality as such. He published three major works: *Initiation Into Hermetics*, *The Practice of Magical Evocation* and *The Key to the True Quabbalah*, of which the second is by far the most significant. In it Bardon outlined a magical universe as detailed and far-reaching as that of the *Lesser Key of Solomon* and *The Sacred Magic of Abra-Melin the Mage*. Even more extraordinary was his claim that his descriptions of the hierarchy of beings on the inner planes were all the result of personal contact!

Bardon's inner world consists of an astral plane girdling the earth which contains the spirits of the four elements, 360 'heads' of the Zodiac (one for each degree of rotation around the planetary sphere), and the 'Intelligences' of the planets radiating upwards from Earth on the cosmic Tree of Life.

Unlike Georges Chevalier, who is extremely humble in his magical encounters (referring to himself time and time again as a worm before God), Bardon takes the more familiar role of the occultist asserting himself on the inner planes. According to Bardon, the magician is the God-Man. He incarnates the Deity, and this places him spiritually above elementals and planetary beings, who are 'incomplete' (a salamander being only a salamander (fire) and a goblin only a goblin (earth) . . .). Consequently all of the hierarchy are obliged to obey him.

Bardon's method is to imagine himself as God, and then evoke a spirit from a particular sphere. However, the magician must know something of the sphere he is entering, for each is a magical domain with its own specific reality. Bardon's claim is that he has worked his way systematically through the astral framework he presents, using as a magical safeguard his own divinity. The occultist in fact wears a crown to symbolize this purity of intent, and also carries a ritual sword to strike fear into the spirits he encounters. Bardon writes: 'From the days of yore, the secret of magic has been restricted to high castes, potentates, kings and high priests . . . .'[5] The magician as God is, in a sense, reclaiming inner territory as he ventures from one sphere to another.

The realm of elementals provides Franz Bardon with some of his most complete and detailed descriptions. Below are entries for two supernatural entities, Osipeh, a female elemental of Water, and Ordaphe, a gnome of the Earth:

> *Osipeh* – colour of sign: blue – is a most beautiful water spirit and not only a complete ruler over this element, but also of the magic of water. She likes very much to introduce the magician into the rhythm of the water element by the magic of sounds. She is an excellent singer and dancer as are all her subordinate spirits experts in these arts, and they perform the nicest dances and accompany them with lovely songs. If the magician resists the tempting invitations of this female ruler and gets her under his power, she will place at his disposal several spirits subordinate to her. I know from my own experience that she likes to serve the magician who rules her . . . .[6]

> *Ordaphe* – colour for drawing his sign: black – is a mighty king of gnomes. If the magician so wishes, Ordaphe will lead him through his kingdom and show him all the treasures that are under the earth in the form of ore. He too has a great number of gnomes subordinated to him who do the work designated them under the surface of the earth. Some of them guard the ores, others work on their refinement and maintenance. Ordaphe likes to place gnomes at the disposal of the magician (but) . . . he must never use these spirits for avaricious purposes.[7]

We recall that mythologically the four elements are personalized into salamanders (fire), sylphs (air), undines, mermaids or mermen (water) and goblins and gnomes (earth). Franz Bardon's symbolic encounters with these entities occur in a trance-like state on a low level of the astral plane (for the existential magician, the lower reaches of the creative imagination). It is also significant that each entity has a specific sign or sigil, by which it is summoned. This is coloured appropriately: Earth = black; Water = blue or silver; Fire = red. (No details are provided by Bardon for Air, since air elements are said to be 'not at all pleased with men', and in view of our current ecological problems with air pollution this is hardly surprising!)

The sigil symbolizes the means of contact and we will encounter this type of ritualized expression again and again in the magical method. In the Golden Dawn system the coloured Tattva cards and the elaborate Enochian squares were similarly used as doorways to specific astral spaces. Once again, we find a correlation between the symbol and the experience of the magician, so that the magical vision, whether of gnomes, undines or whatever, is directly precipitated by the symbol of entry. In a similar way, Franz Bardon provides the sigil for each magical entity as a means of evoking *that one specifically*.

Although Bardon would seem to be implying that the magician has scaled the full range of creation in taking on the mantle of divine authority, this is not really the case. The magician is himself evolving, and for Bardon the process of growth continues as the occultist gains more and more specific knowledge of each of the inner domains open to him. He also makes pacts and alliances with high angels and geniuses, who bestow their blessings and talents upon him.

Bardon's magical universe is such that by virtue of his authority he is free to wander where he will, summoning spirits in the quest for inner knowledge and then sending them back to their proper sphere after the encounter. Bardon follows the system of the Qabalah. His cosmic Tree, which comprises the Zodiac and planetary spheres, grows upward from the Earth and out of the plane of astral elementals which has just been described. Bardon, like many other contemporary magicians is really a shaman. He knows the framework of his inner cosmos, and sees his purpose as venturing on the inner journey up through its levels of being. Its myriad inhabitants have particular qualities which identify them. But providing the magician stands in his magical circle, which symbolizes the divine qualities of the universe, he can come to no harm:[8]

The magician who stands in the centre of the magical circle . . . is in fact, symbolising the Divine in the Universe . . . furthermore, by standing in the centre of the magical circle, the magician also represents the Divine in the microcosm and controls and rules these beings in a totalitarian manner . . . the magician is, at that instant, a perfect magic authority whom all powers and spirits must absolutely obey . . . .

Bardon's method stresses that it is the magician who is in control. Failure to dominate an invoked entity may lead to spirit possession. (Again, in existential terms, this is to allow a forceful mental image to dominate the psychic processes, having wrenched it symbolically out of the creative imagination.)

On the other hand, by assuming the function of divine authority, the magician has open to him all of the spheres and planes of manifestation, together with their varied inhabitants. He is a potential master of them all.

While occultists like Franz Bardon and Georges Chevalier can be fairly stated to have worked ouside the occult 'mainstream', the cosmology of the Hermetic Order of the Golden Dawn has had a significant impact on the 'new consciousness' which has emerged as a post-psychedelic phenomenon. Although Eastern systems of thought like *The Tibetan Book of the Dead*, the *I Ching* and certain tracts from the Zen literature captured the imagination of the 1960s counter-culture in its exploration of drug states and peak experiences, it was not long after that the Tarot and Magic became identified as Western equivalents of these mystical philosophies. The influential, though frequently inaccurate, *Morning of the Magicians* of Louis Pauwels and Jacques Bergier, first published in 1960, had already pointed to the existence of the Golden Dawn society as a major esoteric group concerned with charting the potentials of the magical imagination. Later, Aleister Crowley's face showed up alongside Edgar Allan Poe's and many others, on the collage cover of the Beatles' popular psychedelic *Sergeant Peppers* album and the notorious activities of the Manson cult were characteristic of a fascination with occult literature at this time. Anton La Vey, the San Francisco warlock, appeared meanwhile as the Devil in *Rosemary's Baby*.

But there were more wholesome interests too. Arthur Waite's *Rider* Tarot pack has held perennial fascination, and many of his other works, notably *The Holy Kabbalah*, *The Brotherhood of the Rosy Cross* and his interpretation of the Tarot, which accompanied the pack of cards, were reissued in the 1960s in the United States, as symptomatic of the renewed interest. Israel Regardie's reprinted, edited versions of numerous Crowley works were not far behind.

Since this time, magic has found its way into the lives of pop musicians, psychedelic artists and the suburban populace in general. Sociologists have identified the present occult revival as a predominantly middle-class phenomenon.[9]

It is not surprising that the Golden Dawn model of the magical universe should have had wide-ranging impact, for although it has only recently been subject to thorough historical documentation, the Society first undertook the investigation of the mythological psyche in 1888, and this period in history saw new breakthroughs in the perception of man as a creative being.

Noted psychiatrist, Silvano Arieti, in his recent book *Creativity*, writes that 'it was in 1895 that Freud and Breuer published their book on hysteria which marked the beginning of the psychoanalytic era and opened the road to the study of the unconscious . . . .'[10] He also notes that in the same year Cezanne held his first exhibition of modern 'primitive' paintings which marked a turning away from styles that reproduced nature, and showed instead a preoccupation with the identity and essence of depicted objects. Visionary modes of art like Cubism and Surrealism followed soon after.

Historically the Golden Dawn followed in the tradition of the European Rosicrucian and Masonic esoteric schools, and the writings of European occultists like Papus and Eliphas Lévi were interpreted with interest by Waite and Crowley, the latter claiming Lévi as a former incarnation.

But the scope of the Golden Dawn was far broader than that of its predecessors and no occult society since has been able to muster the prodigious range of talent that passed through its ranks: writers of the calibre of W. B. Yeats, scientists like the Astronomer Royal for Scotland, William Peck, and doctors like Wynn Westcott and Edward Berridge. Ithell Colquhoun's *Swords of Wisdom* and Ellic Howe's *Magicians of the Golden Dawn*, which document the society, are perhaps the two most authoritative histories of the Order that have yet been produced.

Our concern here however is more with the nature of the magical universe envisaged in the Golden Dawn by its founders and practitioners. More than to any other person the group owes the scope of its magical vision to one man: Samuel Liddell MacGregor Mathers (1854-1918).

It had been common until Mathers's time for occultists and magicians

20

to work single, specific systems. We can turn to Cornelius Agrippa's alchemical treatises, Edward Kelley's skrying in trance and communicating with angels and Francis Barrett's idiosyncratic magical system, *The Magus, or Celestial Intelligencer* (1801). We find Papus concerned primarily with the origins of Tarot symbolism, Robert Fludd, medieval artist par excellence, infatuated with Rosicrucian imagery, and Thomas Vaughan engaged in a form of tantric alchemy.

Mathers proposed that the Western magician should investigate all the cosmologies of his cultural tradition. In 1887 he published the first English translation of Knorr Von Rosenroth's *Kabbala Denudata*, and from it isolated as a major workable framework, the motif of the Tree of Life. His masonic background, and that of his founding colleagues, presupposed an interest in the Egyptian mysteries, which several Masonic authorities claimed as a formative source. Mathers's father was of Scottish descent and, like Yeats, Mathers was fascinated by the Celtic tradition. He was also a member of the pre-Golden Dawn group *Societas Rosicruciana in Anglia* which claimed spiritual connections with Continental Rosicrucianism. The ground of eclecticism was laid. Mathers was a self-taught scholar with a sound knowledge of French, Latin and Greek, and some Coptic and Hebrew. He was later to preoccupy himself in translating a number of key magical documents which might otherwise have been doomed to obscurity in museum archives.

The significance of this wide range of interests was that the magical rituals of the Golden Dawn, in whose shaping and formation Mathers played a major role came to draw on every major mythology in Western culture.

Consequently what we may term the Golden Dawn cosmology was a very elaborate one indeed, and whereas Franz Bardon's relatively narrow system was based on the Qabalah and a hierarchy of elementals and planetary spirits, Mathers and his colleagues undertook a vast comparative study.

The scope of the magical framework in question is provided by a work entitled 777, and published by Aleister Crowley as solely his own work. The book is in fact a series of annotated tables of symbols, images and ascriptions which show cross-correlations between religious and magical pantheons, perfumes, minerals, plants and imaginary beings. In his editorial preface to the book, Israel Regardie puts forward the highly unlikely claim that 'Crowley, who had a phenomenal memory, wrote it at Bournemouth in a week without reference books . . ..' *777*, at any rate, *was* published privately by Crowley in 1909.[11]

Ithell Colquhoun is of the opinion that Crowley and his friend Allan Bennett, both of whom were disciples of Mathers, borrowed the material, at least in part, from their teacher. She notes that a manuscript entitled *The Book of Correspondences*, was circulated among senior Golden Dawn students in the 1890s. There is certainly some thematic evidence in her favour, for if we examine Crowley's Tarot ascriptions as one example, we find that he has opted for what we might call the 'traditional' listing. Readers familiar with his Thoth pack will know that Crowley in fact tampered considerably with the symbolism of these cards – converting the card of *Strength* into *Lust* and depicting the Whore of Babylon for example – and in particular he reversed the cards of *The Emperor* and *The Star* in their positions on the Tree of Life. This was in line with his philosophy that 'Every man and woman is a star . . .', which had become a key feature of his magical philosophy since his conversion to Egyptian-based sexual magic in 1904.

Basically *777* uses as its core framework the ten levels of consciousness of the Qabalistic Tree of Life, and the twenty-two interconnecting paths (normally represented by the Major Tarot trumps). Regardie calls the book 'a Qabalistic dictionary of ceremonial magic, oriental mysticism, comparative religion and symbology . . . a handbook for ceremonial invocation and for checking the validity of dreams and visions'.[12] Certainly it is all these things. But from the viewpoint of the purpose of this book I would like to re-state the argument slightly and suggest that *777* represents the parameters of the modern magical imagination.

The construct of the Tree is in itself a cosmological metaphor which describes the hierarchy of energy levels in the manifested universe. The Tree embraces the range of being from finite, material reality through to infinite inner space. The magician following on its pathways grows in spiritual consciousness as he ascends the Tree, and a variety of methods are open to him. He may meditate on each sphere, rise on the inner planes in trance, or simulate the levels of consciousness imaginatively in ritual. The Tree by itself, as a Jewish mystical symbol, had a monotheistic base however. Mathers and his magical colleagues found that they were able to correlate other mythologies, and poly-theistic ones at that, with the levels on the Tree.

The most important correspondences in *777* are thus the tables of deities listed as equivalents in different pantheons. This was an early attempt to cross-correlate archetypes, and the range of comparison was wide indeed. It is here that Regardie may well be right in ascribing certain Oriental sections to Crowley. Crowley travelled widely in the East and it is likely that the Hindu and Chinese listings were his own work.

When we assemble some of the data of 777 we arrive at something like the following:

Level	Qabalah	Astrology	Egyptian	Greek
1	Kether	Primum Mobile	Harpocrates	Zeus
2	Chokmah	Zodiac/Fixed Stars	Ptah	Uranus
3	Binah	Saturn	Isis	Demeter
4	Chesed	Jupiter	Amoun	Poseidon
5	Geburah	Mars	Horus	Ares
6	Tiphareth	Sol	Ra	Apollo
7	Netzach	Venus	Hathor	Aphrodite
8	Hod	Mercury	Anubis	Hermes
9	Yesod	Luna	Shu	Diana
10	Malkuth	The Elements	Seb	Persephone

Hindu	Precious Stones	Perfumes
Parabrahm	Diamond	Ambergris
Shiva	Star Ruby, Turquoise	Musk
Sakti	Star Sapphire, Pearl	Myrrh, Civet
Indra	Amethyst	Cedar
Varuna, avatar	Ruby	Tobacco
Vishnu-Hari-Krishna-Rama	Topaz	Olibanum
—	Emerald	Benzoin, Rose, Sandlewood
Hanuman	Opal	Storax
Ganesha	Quartz	Jasmine
Lakshmi	Rock Crystal	Dittany of Crete

The listings in 777 are of course much more extensive than this and further headings include Scandinavian gods, Buddhist meditations, plants, magical weapons, mineral and vegetable drugs, and the letters of the Greek, Arabic and Coptic alphabets.

The importance of 777 lies in the fact that it was the first attempt in the literature to systematize the various images said to occur at different levels of expanded consciousness. The perfumes and stones listed above were intended as appropriate ritual objects in keeping with the qualities of the invoked god.

When we consider that Freud's initial inroads into the unconscious were in terms of uncovering repressed sexual drives, it is interesting plotting this discovery on the Tree of Life, particularly when we remember that the magicians similarly regarded the Tree as a symbol of the unconscious mind. On the Tree of Man – the archetypal Adam Kadmon is superimposed so that Kether is his crown, Malkuth his feet – we find that Yesod symbolizes the sexual genital region. On a comparative basis, Luna is an appropriate symbol for the monthly cycle in woman and Diana is Queen of the witches with their fertility worship. Freud's interpretation of the subconscious, by virtue of its dominating sexual emphasis, is thus symbolically based on Yesod. Jung, by comparison delved deeper into the psyche and evolved his theory of individuation – making oneself whole. His emphasis on inner harmony, on the universal symbol of the mandala (or cosmic disc) and on spiritual rebirth, are all appropriate to Tiphareth, the centre of the Tree and 'hub of the wheel'.

Arieti has highlighted Freud's achievement in the 1890s but it is clear that at the same time the magicians of the Golden Dawn were endeavouring to chart parallel mythological processes in the psyche using the method of the direct encounter.

777 was compiled gradually and slowly, as the result of visionary explorations of the Order's membership, and by careful examination of the themes in comparative mystical literature. It built very extensively on the important, but simple, correlation suggested by Eliphas Lévi of the ten Sephiroth of the Tree and the twenty-two Major Tarot Trumps. As I shall demonstrate subsequently, the Tarot is in itself a profound mythology incorporating all the classical themes of transformation. The framework of the Tree would be bare without it.

There is no question that the above magical correlations have caused anger in certain academic circles. In his most recent work, Gershom Scholem writes: 'the activities of French and English occultists contributed nothing and only served to create considerable confusion between the teachings of the Kabbalah and their own totally unrelated inventions such as the alleged Kabbalistic origin of the Tarot cards . . . .'[13]

No informed occultist does of course claim a Kabbalistic *origin* for these cards. What has been suggested, and certainly verified by mystical practice in recent years, is that different religious belief systems overlap in their content. The view in the Golden Dawn was that by correlating common themes in mystical teachings they became more universal in their impact. While the essential individuality of each framework of belief was respected, cross-comparison of the kind undertaken above pointed to the non-exclusiveness of any one school of thought. The belief in the non-exclusiveness of one's beliefs brings with it an attitude of tolerance. By comparison, the political effect of any given heresy is such that, as an alternative belief system, it is often brutally decried on the grounds of its posing a threat to the dominant and therefore 'exclusive' belief systems. The following remarks by Heinrich Zimmer indicate the mythological importance of what was actually a persecuted heretical doctrine in medieval Europe:[14]

> It is my belief that the pictorial script of these [Tarot] face cards represented the degrees of an esoteric order of initiation; employing largely Christian signs, but masking the formulae of the heretical Gnostic teaching that was so widespread in Southern France up to the fifteenth century. The initiate, passing through twenty degrees of gradually amplifying enlightenment and beset by as many characteristic temptations, at last arrived at the stage of a mystical union with the Holy Trinity and this is what was symbolized in the culminating image of the series 'The Dancing Hermaphrodite'. The Soul was the bride of the Lord, the figure of the Hermaphrodite; the two were one. The figure is immediately suggestive of the Dancing Shiva; Shiva unites in himself the Female and the Male. Such a bisexual symbol represents the embodiment in a single form all the pairs of opposites, a transcendence of the contraries of phenomenality; and this incarnate form of forms is then conceived of as the One whose dance is the created world.

Considerable space has been devoted to the Tarot in a subsequent chapter with a view to examining the initiatory themes present in the Tarot symbolism. However, it is apparent that the Golden Dawn method rose above the popular conception of 'magic' and attempted to systematize the same inner realms of the psyche as those investigated by classical psychoanalysis.

There is no doubt that the Golden Dawn system employed trial and error. The ceremonial magicians were required to keep magical diaries of their experiences of encounters with supernatural entities on various of the inner paths. As certain 'constants' emerged, specific deities and images were 'allocated a position on the Tree'. It was at this stage that what began as a quest for archetypes became an affirmation of a particular magical 'programme'. These aspects are discussed in a subsequent comparison of the thought of Carl Jung and John Lilly, for both have relevance to the understanding of the magical process.

The structure of the magical journey

The Tree of Life is the integral framework used in contemporary magic for expanding consciousness. The standard form of interconnecting the ten spheres or *sephiroth* on the Tree is given in the diagram on p. 65. This symbol is a visual metaphor which describes the mystical Judaic macrocosm – the process of God becoming real in the world through the process of unfolded creation. As indicated above, with the super-imposition of Adam Kadmon upon the Tree, it also comes to represent man's capacity for discovering his spiritual source – *his essential ground of being*.

As Gershom Scholem and other contemporary writers – among them Z'evben Shimon Halevi and Leo Schaya – have shown the Qabalah is of course a complete system in itself and does not need the Tarot. By the same token, modern ceremonial magic has opted to include it in its eclectic methodology and has similarly experimented with different means of interconnecting the Paths upon the Tree. Traditionally the Tree is the result of an impulse through 'four worlds' – *Atziluth*: Principles; *Briah*: Creativity; *Yetzirah*: Formative Imagination and *Assiah*: Activities. The four worlds straddle ten levels of being and these can be listed briefly as follows: Atziluth is the world of archetypes, the very essence of creation. Beneath this plane, in Briah, these archetypes begin to crystallize into specific ideas, and in Yetzirah definite forms appear whose familiar counterparts may be found in the archetypal images of the unconscious mind. In the fourth world, Assiah, the manifesting forms of creation finally become real in the sense we know them normally.

The ten spheres of the Tree of Life embrace these four worlds, and man, as the microcosm, thus has a spiritual counterpart at all of these levels. The magician actively seeks knowledge of these inner states and the Tree and its associated paths of the Tarot constitute a framework for exploring transcendental states of consciousness.

Archetypes and belief systems – the relevance of C. G. Jung and John Lilly

It is hardly surprising that in endeavouring to explain magical frameworks psychologically, most contemporary occultists have indicated a preference for the analysis of C. G. Jung. In Jung's writings we discover a remarkably rich synthesis in his treatment of mythology and legend and its relation to the primordial imagery of the psyche. While Jung was probably unaware of the existence of the Golden Dawn, he nevertheless notes that the 'image series of the Tarot cards were descendants of the archetypes of transformation',[1] and he provides, with his conceptual divisions of the psyche into the personal and collective unconscious, an important basis for understanding the workings of the magical imagination.

In Israel Regardie's view man has discovered that 'a barrier of inhibition is built up between the unconscious and conscious thinking self . . . we have become cut off from our roots, and have no power, no ability to contact the deeper, the instinctual, the most potent side of our natures'.[2] For him, the symbolism of magic – with its meditative and ceremonial aids acting as catalysts to the imagination – provides a means of breaking down this barrier. The magician comes to realize this identity and unity with the unconscious self.

I have referred earlier to the shamanistic exploration upon the Tree of Life and also to the related out-of-the-body/trance state which accompanies it. Regardie, like most occultists, identifies the so-called astral planes, the inner mythological domain, with Jung's concept of the collective unconscious.

In *The Structure of the Psyche* Jung claimed that the collective unconscious 'contains the whole spiritual heritage of mankind's evolution born anew in the brain structure of every individual'.[3] Its dominant primordial images he called 'archetypes' – identifying them as the deepest and most profound strata of the mind.

The influential English occultist W. E. Butler, who trained under Dion Fortune in the Fraternity of the Inner Light, commented on the parallels between the Collective Unconscious and the magician's cosmological territory: 'Magic, with its roots in the immemorial past . . . speaks to the subconscious mind of man through the archaic images of its symbols and rituals and thereby provides those "changes in consciousness" which the magician seeks.'[4] Butler is here referring to Dion Fortune's definition of magic as the technique of changing one's consciousness subject to will. The magical aim is to explore and integrate the universal imagery of the psyche which is symbolic of the higher self.

Jung regarded the Collective Unconscious as 'objective' – it was able to resist the artificial ordering processes conceived by the personal consciousness. And yet the 'universal' domain has for many remained unacknowledged as a source of inner stability.

As contemporary writers like Theodore Roszak and Stephen Larsen have noted, modern man – with his hankering for gurus and spiritual therapy – seems to be expressing a need to reaffirm his contact with these 'sacred' realms of being. If the present occult revival is a symptom of this need, it is understandable that the Golden Dawn system of magic and Jung's formulation of the mythological unconscious should embrace similar territory.

Jolande Jacobi, in a concise exposition of Jung's views on archetypes writes:[5]

In every single individual psyche they can awaken to new life, exert their magic power and condense into a kind of 'individual mythology' which presents an impressive parallel to the great traditional mythologies of all peoples and epochs, concretizing as it were, their origin, essence and meaning and throwing new light on them . . . . The archetype as the primal source of all human experience lies in the unconscious, whence it reaches into our lives. Thus it becomes imperative to resolve its projections, to raise its contents to consciousness.

MacGregor Mathers and his colleagues in the Golden Dawn were quick to perceive the implications of the Tarot and Qabalah as a means for plumbing these normally unconscious depths. Their ritual activity was specifically orientated initially to awakening in each of the Golden Dawn members an awareness of the four lowest mythological sephiroth on the Tree of Life. This was followed – at the more advanced stages of initiation in the so-called Second Order – by the ceremony culminating in the attainment of Tiphareth or rebirth consciousness. Tiphareth may be regarded as the centre of a mandala delineated upon the Qabalistic Tree. As a state of consciousness associated with spiritual rebirth, the magician awakens in his own consciousness the sense of the God-man. Tiphareth is a symbol both of transformation and individuation. It is a transformatory experience in the sense that it leads higher up the Middle Pillar to universal consciousness – the state devoid of all notions of individuality – but it is also an important stage in individuation as the centre of the mandala of inner man. As Edward Edinger has said, 'individuation is a process not a realised goal. Each new level of integration must submit to further transformation. . . .'[6] The shaman does not rest in Tiphareth – he pushes on further up the Tree.

It is this sense of spiritual evolution – expressed in Jung's work as the search for inner wholeness – which again characteristically links his psychological model to that of modern magic.

According to Butler, 'It is here that the fourth instinct (i.e. the Religious Instinct) posited by Jung comes in, for it is the counterpole drawing the developing man up to greater heights and we might with advantage equate this fourth drive with what the occultists call the Superconscious or Higher Self.'[7] Dion Fortune similarly regarded 'the Microcosmic Archetypes – such as the Father, Mother, Magician and wise women (as representing) the linking of the developing soul with certain "lines of force" in the macrocosm, or in other words, the bringing of the manhood to God or the Gods.'[8] She followed Jung in characterizing these archetypes as 'objective' – as intrinsic symbolic vortexes in the psyche, representative of 'creative evolution'.

A study of the Tarot, especially, reveals a mix of all of Jung's dominant archetypes. As aspects of the Great Father we find *The Emperor*, *The Hierophant* and *The Charioteer*, while the Great Mother is represented by *The Empress*, *Justice* and as Mother Nature subduing the Lion or *Strength*. The Divine Child is found expressed in both polarities with the dancing children of *The Sun* and *The Lovers*. The Divine Maiden is depicted on *The Star*, *The World* and *The High Priestess*, just as the Trickster – whom Jung describes as 'the forerunner of the saviour, and like him God, man and animal at once' – is superbly portrayed in the form of *The Devil*. A master of delusion, the Devil, with his sagging breast and hairy torso is a mockery of the Divine Hermaphrodite. The archetype of the Wise Old Man 'who penetrates the chaotic darkness of mere life with the light of meaning' is shown in the form of *The Hermit* who treads towards the Void holding his shining lantern.

Jung refers to symbols as 'transformers of energy'[9] and he distinguishes symbols from signs, which are dead, secular representations without any connotation of mystery.

The meditative trance method of the Tattvas, the Enochian squares and the Tarot which will be discussed subsequently, is such that the magician chooses a path of entry which precipitates a specific mythological process – a visionary encounter with the Gods upon the Tree. The inner symbolic domain entered by this means is undoubtedly directly related to the nature of the symbolic doorway. As such these cards take on the same function as a mandala – they are what Jung calls 'a centering effect' for concentration – 'they not only express order, they also bring it about.'[10] The entire notion of *magical order and control* – of choosing a specific Tarot card, of invoking god-names for protection, of remaining within the magical circle (another mandala symbol) and of banishing chaos (evil) as a prelude to ceremonial – such controls are designed to integrate all of the magician's psychic experiences into his consciousness, subject to his will.

Jolande Jacobi notes that any such union, whether through ritual enactment or by shamanistic trance, with archetypal sources, constitutes an evolutionary expansion of consciousness. 'If once the transformed individual has recognized himself as "God's image and likeness" in the deepest sense, the sense of ethical obligation, he will, as Jung says, become "on one side a being of superior wisdom, on the other a being of superior will".'[11]

It may be appropriate to retrace, in the Jungian sense, the archetypal domain of the contemporary magician. At the core of the magical cosmology we find a four-fold division of archetypes into FATHER-MOTHER-SON-DAUGHTER which is often said to be based on the four-fold sacred name of God, JHVH. Within the monotheistic framework of the Tree of Life it becomes possible to correlate other mythologies. The two most complete pantheons, which provided the dominant inspiration for ceremonial magic and meditative purposes in the Golden Dawn, were the Egyptian and the Graeco-Roman. The creation process in the Qabalah is regarded as one of gradual development, while in ancient Greece with the interrelations of so many of the gods the process was necessarily less linear. And whereas on the Tree itself the level of earth consciousness is the *end-result* of the cosmic process, in Egyptian mythology the creation occurs as a result of the separation of the earth and the sky. Consequently, although there are correlations of archetypes they do not always arise in the same sequence in their respective mythologies.

30

The magical cosmology of the Tree of Life is as follows:

KETHER — The first manifestation of creation from the Infinity of non-existence beyond. Transcendent above the duality of good and evil, male and female or force and form, this profound state of cosmic consciousness is symbolized mythologically by the Divine Hermaphrodite.

CHOKMAH and BINAH — As the great impulses of force and form these emanations are symbolized by the Great Father, who provides the spark or sperm of creative manifestation, and the Great Mother who is the womb of the World. Their cosmic marriage is a sacred mystery however, for as a conjunction they complete the Trinity and remain beyond the actual workings of the created universe itself.

The remaining sephiroth are the Seven Days of Creation headed by a 'lower' (or more manifest) aspect of the Father archetype who acts as guardian of the world.

In CHESED and GEBURAH he shows his two dynamic aspects of Mercy and Severity, revealing the universe to be an ongoing process of life, destruction and renewal.

TIPHARETH is the consciousness level of the God-man — the divine Son who mythologically encompasses the Sun and the process of spiritual rebirth.

NETZACH is one of three subsequent emanations which reflect in mythological terms lesser aspects of the Great Mother and in turn are linked to the Moon. Netzach represents emotional love and equates with the love of the divine Son for the world.

The other feminine levels of consciousness are the ninth and tenth sephiroth YESOD and MALKUTH which come to represent the sexual instincts and the fertile earth itself.

HOD, the eighth sephiroth, like Tiphareth, is a 'lower' masculine form — and bears a strong relation to Chokmah. Its deities are often messengers of the gods — intermediaries between transcendence and physical reality.

In the sense that the shaman or magician is entering the inner domain at the level of earth consciousness in order to proceed to the more transcendental states, the sequence is now reversed.

First level

MALKUTH   Associated with crops, the harvest and the living environment, this sphere is closely related to gods of vegetation, especially in their seasonal, cyclic aspects. In Egyptian mythology the representative deity was Geb, with mountains and valleys forming the undulations of his body. In Greece the myth of Persephone went beyond the representation of the actual world in relating the life–death polarity of the wheat grain cycle. Snatched into the underworld by Hades/Aidoneus, Persephone later spent the winter months in his realm as the fearsome queen of death and the other six months on earth with Demeter, goddess of the abundant harvest. Persephone thus symbolizes the growth and decay of the cereal crop itself.

YESOD is the seat of the sexual instinct, called Nephesch in the Qabalah and linked to lunar myths of fertility. In Egypt, Isis is the wife of the solar deity Osiris and is a great magical enchantress and healer. She recreates the phallus of the slain Osiris and gives birth to Horus by him. The Greek lunar deity meanwhile had three faces – as Selene (the Moon), as Artemis (goddess of the witches and guardian of herbal, medicinal secrets) and as Hecate, who as scourge of the underworld was sometimes combined with the dark face of Persephone.

HOD equates with intellect, rational thought and order, and mythologically has come to be linked with Thoth and Hermes who were themselves combined as deities during the Greek period in ancient Egypt. Thoth is the inventor of speech, the divine intelligence, a great magician and the scribe and representative of the gods. He also has some connections with the Moon – which is mythologically dominant as a symbol on this part of the Tree. Thoth in his aspect of interrelating with the world may be ascribed to Hod, as can Anubis the jackal god of death. Anubis was the offspring of Osiris, the Sun-god (the moon similarly reflecting the Sun as a child reflects it parent). Hermes also had connections with the dead, one of his tasks being to conduct the deceased souls to Hades.

On the Tarot card *Judgment* which joins Malkuth and Hod and which forms a triangular aspect with Yesod we are shown human beings rising forth form their tombs to the note of a heraldic trumpet. Mantric sound and transition through death – which itself is symbolic of the lower unconscious mind – are notable features both of Hod and the lower mythological domain upon the Tree.

NETZACH, with its focus on love and emotions, counterbalances the less subjective and more orderly forms associated with Hod. In Egyptian mythology Isis once again – as the lover and wife of Osiris – and Hathor with her symbol of the solar disc, are female counterparts of the solar god. Nephthys, the wife of Osiris' tyrannous brother Set, presents with her husband the dark face of these two archetypes and both reflect to some extent Jung's concept of the 'trickster' archetype. Aphrodite as the Greek goddess of love and beauty, was said to have been born in the ocean foam near the island of Cythera. But just as Netzach is a development from the sexual regions of Yesod, so too is Aphrodite a sensuous lover. She has numerous amours with Ares, Hermes, Dionysus, Anchises and others. She is also representative of the reproductive powers in nature and as such is a lower form of the Great Mother – the Womb of the Universe.

TIPHARETH is the centre of the Tree, the solar vortex in inner man – the mediating stage between man and godhead on the mystical ascent. A sphere of beauty, life and harmony, Tiphareth is associated with deities of life and light, rebirth and resurrection. It is also the sphere of sacrifice, for the more limited terrestrial personality is now offered by the shaman in place of universal understanding and insight. In Egyptian cosmology the resurrected Osiris, the Sun-god who rules triumphantly over the forms of darkness in the underworld Halls of Judgment, profoundly demonstrates the triumph of renewal. The Greek Helios-Apollo was similarly god of the Sun, healer and destroyer of monsters (the negative forms of existence). He and Artemis are twin brother and sister (sun and moon), just as Geb and Nu (earth and sky) gave rise to Osiris and Isis (sun and moon) in Egyptian cosmology.

GEBURAH is the archetype of the warrior or the wrathful face of the Great Father. Horus, as avenger of his father Osiris' death, became the model for the pharaoh kings. We find his medieval equivalent on *The Charioteer* of the major Tarot arcana. In Greece Ares was god of war, champion of Troy and the lover of Aphrodite. Interestingly, on the Tree of Life Geburah and Netzach form a diagonal balance with one another. There are also elements of an angry Poseidon on *The Charioteer* for he drives his chariot vengefully through the ocean of form – destroying outmoded creation in order to make way for new impulses of life.

CHESED parallels GEBURAH but presents a more passive watchful aspect. Ra, in the Egyptian system, was father of the gods and man-kind – not himself the creator of the universe, but its maintainer. Zeus plays a similar role. While he is not the originator of the world we see him as the most powerful of the gods and respected, despite his numerous procreative activities outside his marriage to Hera, as the embodiment of justice.

Beyond these archetypal areas we begin to move into the domain regarded as the Primal Mystery. The Great Mother and Father are still present as symbolic images although the symbol itself has less relevance in this transcendental region.

BINAH AND CHOKMAH The marriage of Shu (the atmosphere) with Tefnut (life principle) produced the more 'regional' or 'terrestrial' Egyptian deities Osiris and Isis.

Similarly, while Zeus was thought to dominate actual creation, he was himself the son of Cronus and Rhea. Cronus was one of the Titans and Rhea was the 'Great Mother of the Gods'. On the Tree of Life the most exalted stage of consciousness, the Monad, is KETHER – the Crown. Frequently the symbolic image of Kether is hermaphroditic – in alchemy the king and queen wedded into a single body. In the Gnosticism of Basilides the creator god Abraxas contained the polarities of both good and evil.

The cosmology of Heliopolis regarded Atum the creator as being originally bisexual. He later came to be identified with Ra and was symbolized by the Bennu bird or phoenix, a lower-order solar symbol.

In Memphis the creator was Ptah and in Thebes Amon, but invariably the creator was believed to emerge from the infinite space of Nu. In Greek mythology the comparable deity was Ouranos – Father Sky, the most ancient of all the gods who – with Gaea – gave rise to the archetypal parents Cronus and Rhea.

It is clear that these profound mythologies eventually taper off into an ineffable mystery. The consciousness states which these deities represent are part of a system of belief which is open-ended or limitless. In fact the structure of these accumulated mythologies is potentially so vast that it embraces the entire range of inspirational levels, not only of the Western magical imagination, but also of the creative psyche itself.

In so far as any magician seeks to rediscover the actual sources of creative activity he is likely to apply some system of activating these archetypes. Unfortunately the occult tradition has frequently clouded its aims in power struggles and other non-mythological activities. A study of modern occult sources shows all the revealing signs of dogma and literalism which have been decried vigorously as faults in other religious institutions.[12]

All too often magical devotees have been asked to believe in 'adepts and secret chiefs', 'root races', 'angelic and demonic beings, astral vibrations and ritual formulae, without any meaningful explanation of what is really meant by these concepts'.

In view of these tendencies towards dogma it is interesting to note the views of John Lilly who has produced a perceptive exposition, in *Simulations of God*, of the nature of belief itself.

A given archetype – as an image of illumination – may manifest itself in a variety of cultural practices and religious beliefs. If the practitioners of a belief system are sufficiently convinced of the exclusiveness of their own particular expression they may be given to religious crusades, conflicts with rival factions, or other extremist behaviour. Alternatively they may acquire excessive pride and 'devotional smugness' and endeavour to clasp to themselves their secret and sacred truths. One of John Lilly's main avenues of inquiry has been to consider the effect beliefs have on those who adhere to them.

In *Simulations of God* he writes:[13]

> Dogma arises when one asserts the exclusiveness and 'truth' of a specific belief system. Mystical experiences can be used to support dogma . . . to extend into proofs of belief systems. All we are calling to attention here is that if one forms the basic belief that these phenomena originate from a God Out There, from the results of one's use of rituals directed to a God Out There and from a prayer to a God Out There, then one is not exploring all the possibilities . . . .

Lilly raises the important issue that the belief system can act as a constraint upon any insights, intuition or illumination which may arise. In one degree the Tree of Life system *is* an imposition; it becomes less so if we realize its metaphorical symbolic qualities and the essentially mysterious states of being which it delineates.

John Lilly's investigation of belief systems dates from his well-known explorations of transcendental states by means of a sensory-deprivation tank. He investigated the idea that as one's external sources of stimulation are closed off, the mind manifests certain belief patterns which have already been programmed by 'the human biocomputer'. His initial work consisted in charting certain inner spaces – in particular those investigated by Oscar Ichazo and Gurdjieff and detailed in the Arica training, and more recently the Zen states of Franklin Merrell Wolff. His views on the relativity of systems of belief are particularly relevant to the study of magic since for some the symbol of the Tree of Life has acquired the status of an intrinsic attribute of the mind.

Lilly points out that what we are all dealing with is a system of metaphors. The more impressive metaphors span a wide range of consciousness, while the less impressive ones are restrictive, mind-containing, rather than mind-revealing.

35

Mircea Eliade has suggested that the Western mind has a tendency towards 'linear' forms and tends to conceptualize in terms of beginnings and endings whereas the Eastern psyche gives more status to infinite cycles.[14] If Eliade is right, and the Tree of Life (for all its poetic beauty) *is* superficially a mesh of points which define and structure, we are perhaps wise to remember its *intangible* qualities: the Tree is a *metaphor* for imposing order on the chaos of the unconscious. It is ultimately *open-ended* since Kether expands into the infinite Light and Space of Ain Soph Aur. The modern magical Qabalah is itself a system of manipulating symbols but then *casting them into the Void* once their reality is transcended – as seen with the Tarot. *The Fool* is depicted throwing away his possessions and dancing into a chasm of Non-Being.

Lilly writes:[15]

> to remain open-ended one's God must be huge – in order to include one's ignorance, the unknown, the ineffable. Instead of God as the Belief, the Simulation, the Model, one adheres to God as Mystery, God as the Unknown. The explorer of the inner spaces cannot afford the baggage of fixed beliefs. This baggage is too heavy, too limited and too limiting to allow further exploration.

In the contemporary contest the shamanistic magician venturing in the astral domains of the Tree retains a vigilant alertness while not wishing to limit his symbolic ingress. He may meet illuminating or terrifying magical creatures, he may travel through exciting and exotic landscapes or murky elastic limbo states, but it is his belief system – the extent to which he ascribes reality to particular symbolic forms – which will contain him. One imagines as an extreme example, the psychic wanderings of a devout fundamentalist Roman Catholic fearful of the negative side of his belief system – the infinite and immensely painful torment of hell flames licking his flesh. In the sense of John Lilly's explanation he stands trapped by the limit of his belief. Our same devotee automatically passes through the flame imagery when he ascribes non-reality to it, thus making his doctrinal belief open-ended. In the same way, we are reminded of the Avam Samoyed shaman who travels in trance to the domain of the cosmic blacksmith, working a bellows over a huge fire in the bowels of the earth. The shaman is slain and boiled over the fire in a cauldron for 'three years'. The blacksmith then forges him a new head, instructs him in mystical powers and reconstitutes his body. The shaman awakes as a revivified being.[16]

Considered as a perceptual reality in the fantasy realm of trance such a shaman would endure intolerable mental agony if he identified with the dismembering process. Seen however as a rite of transformation in which the shaman dispassionately observes his own rebirth initiation, the process acquires a quite different significance and magical effect. Dismemberment and rebirth are common themes in world mythology. *Death* complements *The Devil* as a predecessor to rebirth in the Tarot arcana and its symbolic content parallels that of our Samoyed shaman. *Death* depicts an angry skeleton wielding a scythe through a crop of human heads. But on closer examination we discover that the skeleton symbolizes the death of negative human limitations; he is hacking away the empty shell of the 'persona'. The 'essence' of each apparently dismembered being flows onwards in the sanctified stream of life towards the inner sun of Tiphareth.

Seen as an end in itself – a ghastly inner hell of wanton destruction – the symbolic location of *Death* is indeed horrific. Viewed as a path of transformation it takes a different perspective. The shaman does not impose a limit to his magical perception and, instead of identifying with the incarcerated body, flows with the stream into a different – and in this case revivifying – domain.

It is the act of symbolic re-emergence, the re-fortification of the shaman himself, which makes him a new man. In psychological terms he has come through his rite of passage as an integrated personality rather than as a schizophrenic. Silvano Arieti, writing on the distinction to be drawn between schizophrenics and mystics, notes:[17]

> The hallucinatory and delusional experiences of the schizophrenic are generally accompanied by a more or less apparent disintegration of the whole person. Religious and mystical experiences seem instead to result in a strengthening and enriching of the personality.

Accordingly, the shaman's role is one of emerging whole. In Jung's terminology this is the core of the individuation process; within Lilly's framework the mystical programme is effective because it takes the shaman into a space where he overcomes his limit – his terrestrial personality – and is reborn into the cosmos.

The programme and the means of entry

While Lilly has acknowledged his indebtedness to Jung, there is an important distinction of emphasis between them. In Jung's work the archetypes are intrinsic; they are profound universal images imbedded in the psyche of man irrespective of his cultural determinants. The latter merely clothe each archetype with an outer form intelligible to the culture concerned, and manifest accordingly in religious and mystical beliefs.

It was the parallel idea that world mythologies correlate which gave rise in the Golden Dawn to the creation of the tables of reference found in 777.

With Lilly, intrinsic constants, or universals *per se*, are not the key factor. What is more important is the range of consciousness made possible by a set of symbols. He asks: 'What are the *limits* of belief – then these are limits to be transcended.' Characteristically in his studies he has chosen especially open-ended cosmologies as his basis – the Zen system in particular. In Lilly's view it is not so important to indicate the existence of specific archetypes, such as the God-man, as to ensure that they are part of the programme adopted for the venture into the inner domain. Without symbols of transformation for example, a programme for inner space would be especially barren.

In this sense the endeavour in 777 to correlate, for example, the hexagrams of the *I Ching* with the Qabalah and the Tarot and a myriad of other symbols, misses the point. While it is valuable to be aware of correlating mythologies, each set of symbols is distinctive to itself. Each taken as a pathway *may* cover comparable territory, but in the long run the shaman must choose one language of symbolism in which to converse or else his communication becomes gibberish. To attempt to conglomerate elements of the *I Ching*, Tarot and Norse mythology as parallel processes has the potential effect of introducing chaos into the programme and disrupts each system's unique expression of the universal process.

Lilly's direction is, it would seem, long overdue in the domain of occult practice. The Western magical tradition is extraordinarily diverse, embracing as it does elements as far reaching as the notorikon and gematria in the Qabalah, coagulation and distillation in spiritual alchemy, the cosmology of Christian Rosencreutz and the medieval symbolism of the Tarot. Lilly asks us by implication to make a choice – if these magical elements do embrace the same inner terrain of the psyche, why clutter the programme? Why feed repetitive symbolic data into the human biocomputer? Why attempt to assimilate a vast mass of esoteric lore, from the intricacies of Enochian grammar through to the 72-letter sacred name of God? – when in fact all we are after is the state of consciousness which takes us through the process of rebirth and 'emergence'.

I have indicated earlier that modern magical procedure, in effect, programmes the imagination. An earth Tattva symbol produces visions of earth – in all likelihood involving anthropomorphic goblin forms such as are described in the writings of Franz Bardon.

In the *Dyadic Cyclone*, John Lilly describes the effects of consciously working within a state of coma produced by a fall in a bicycle accident. Lilly found himself able to focus meditatively in this comatose condition and used as an entry symbol the inverted ⅂ motif found in Spencer Brown's mathematical treatise *The Laws of Form*. This symbol in mathematical terms symbolizes a type of stress point between containment (the inner area of the symbol) and non-containment (the area beyond it) which Lilly refers to as the 'marked' and 'unmarked' states. As with the magical paths of entry, Lilly found himself in trance entering a space linked to his focusing symbol.

The marked state induced a perceptual experience of a specific planet in space where catastrophic, self-destructive wars were occurring – emblematic of a limited, non-organic point of view. The unmarked state produced by his dualistic symbol gave rise, on the other hand, to an experience of the Void – 'of vast inner SPACE'. He found himself travelling as if at sub-atomic levels from one universe to another in regions where 'space itself is indeterminate'. By its very nature Lilly's focusing sigil ⅂ was able to produce each of these polar possibilities.[18]

In comparing the approaches of Jung and Lilly and their relevance to understanding the magical imagination it is clear that a different sense of value may be ascribed to each. Jung indicates the depth and universality of the primordial imagery which is the terrain of the shaman's venture inwards. Lilly, on the other hand, lays emphasis on the range of consciousness offered by any set of symbols and provides in turn the essence of a technique. Once the shaman is assured that his chosen path embraces archetypes of transformation, his programme of entry can be as simple and as clear-minded as required. As a study of the Tarot shows, Tiphareth as a rebirth state may be reached by passage through just two symbolic inner spaces – represented by *The World* and *Temperance*. The role of the magician is to endeavour to build up his perception of the alternative reality presented by these symbols and, then, transcend them. In Lilly's work we find an important implication – that it is not necessary to programme esoteric complexity into the human biocomputer. We also have the option of 'authentic' simplicity.

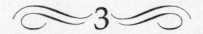

The Tarot and transformation

All shamans, whether in Siberia, Indonesia or Middle America have an operative model of the universe. It may be a cosmic vault upheld by a tree on whose out reaching branches gods and spirits dwell . . . or a hierarchy of supernatural entities each of whom exerts a particular influence on the world.

Similarly, the Qabalistic Tree of Life and the symbolism of the Major Tarot Trumps constitute the operative universe of the Western magician. This framework delineates the symbolic layering of energies within the magical unconscious. The framework asserts: the gods of mythology are inside the head . . . they are themselves a programme. To re-enact the programme is to encounter the gods of the Western tradition, in a certain sequence which is indicative of their sacred power.

If we look at the twenty-two cards of the Major Arcana from *The World* through to *The Fool* in this way we can detect a process of transformation occurring in the impact of the symbols themselves. *The World* and *Judgment* for example are clearly cards of *entry*. The Persephone symbolism of *The World*, the dancing maiden within the wheat wreath — the polarity of life and death as possibilities, the Eleusian promise of spiritual rebirth and awakening — all of these are indicative of greater things to come. Persephone herself was snatched down through the earth into the underworld . . . in modern terms a transition from the real to the unconstricted dimension of dreams.

The 'higher cards' of the Major Arcana, like *The Emperor* and *The Charioteer*, *The Hermit* and *The Hierophant*, are all faces or facets of the great male archetype, just as the *High Priestess* and *The Empress* are embodiments of the great White Goddess before and after procreation.

The Western magician believes that by visualizing the cards inwardly so that they in fact become alive — an inner living process — he is activating archetypal energies. The magician is also introducing a crucial component of the shamanistic act, the concept of *altering consciousness under will.*[1] The magical act is not arbitrary – it is made in the spirit of command. The Western magician knows the scope of his hierarchy of gods and goddesses, his spirit allies and archangels, and when he invokes them he does so within a symbolic confine which defines the space of their activity. He may seek their uplifting energy by invoking them into his own body, but he is very conscious of what he is doing, and imposes the symbolic 'limits' of the effects he is unleashing. The path inward is carefully constructed. Randomness is indicative of a lack of resolve and, in the medieval sense, an invitation to possession – not in terms of an attack by wilful spirits or the devil, so much as dominance by powerful images which impress the explorer by their 'reality'. The magician treads warily through his inner heavens and hells. His weapons are sacred mantras or god-names which within his own 'programme' are of profound significance. The name of a god is superior to that of an elemental by virtue of their very positions in the magical hierarchy. The magician's weapons also include the skilful use of the imagination. Shamans in the West have long known that the imagination is itself a form of direction – it can lead one into wonderful and awesome spaces that are both illuminating and terrifying.

Once again, the shaman in the West employs imagination subject to will. He imposes upon the vast range of visual and auditory possibilities that occur in the hallucinatory world of the lower unconscious, a particular set of images. He follows the set of Tarot symbols not because of their literal value, but because they are internally consistent. They are a visually expressed programme for expanding consciousness through archetypal levels. This provides the magician's sense of certainty. He knows the milestones of his inner territory. It follows that we should not become too entwined in debates concerning the relative validity of Gautama Buddha's eight-fold path compared with the ten Qabalistic sephiroth, or argue about the colours ascribed to the chakras in yoga and in Western magic. There is no escaping the fact that there are minor differences. What is more pertinent is that once we opt, for reasons of temperament or cultural preference, for one particular system, we should abide by the language of its symbolism. In mystical systems we are dealing with elaborate metaphysical metaphors which have implied but not literal validity. Each person has the right to follow his own programme.

There has been much romantic speculation concerning the origin of the Tarot cards. Most commonly the cards have been linked with the gypsies of Central Europe, although the *tarocchi* cards are known to have been present in Italy a hundred years before the incursion of the gypsies around AD 1400. Paul Christian exemplifies a commonly held occult belief that the Tarot cards of the Major Arcana formed a symbolic rendition of an ancient Egyptian initiation rite supposedly held in vaults below the Great Pyramid, and the French theologian Court de Gebelin argued similarly that the word 'Tarot' itself derived from an Egyptian phrase meaning 'royal road of life'.[2]

While it is quite apparent that Tarot symbolism is very much a product of the medieval world-view, with its armoured warriors, castles and ornate costumes, it is also true that whereas the Tarot has no apparent historical links with the earlier cultures of the ancient Near East, and classical Greece and Rome, it does nevertheless embody a similar attempt to explain metaphorically the essential mystery of man's being.

We have stressed that as a system of entry into the psyche the Tarot takes a major place because, as will be shown, the symbols of the twenty-two cards represent a process of transformation. The shaman opening the doors to these energy levels finds himself unable to resist transforming also, as he comes to embody the spiritual energies inherent in each level.

There were however *three* programmes of entry to out-of-the-body consciousness in the Golden Dawn, and as a prelude to describing the Tarot symbolism it is appropriate that we should also consider the other related systems, namely those of the so-called Tattvas and Enochian symbols.

The Tattvas

These are the Hindu symbols of the elements, and represent one of the few Eastern sources of Western magical technique. They are named as follows:

Tejas, a red equilateral Triangle	/	Fire
Apas, a silver crescent	/	Water
Vayu, a blue circle	/	Air
Prithivi, a yellow square	/	Earth
Akasa, a black or indigo egg	/	Spirit (the Void of Space)

The magicians of the Golden Dawn used these symbols for focusing on the mythological spaces defined by the elements, both as individual symbols and in combination. The motifs were mounted on white cards and the magician stared concentratedly at the symbol before averting his gaze to produce an after-image. This was then used as a meditative centering through which to enter the astral planes.

Several visionary accounts of this form of trance entry survive in what have been called the Flying Rolls, documented by Francis King.[3] They usually take the form of encounters with angelic or elemental beings, each said to belong to a specific 'realm' and resemble those described in the earlier section which dealt with the cosmology of Franz Bardon. The visions are frequently of earth spirits, sylphs of the air, undines, fire-beings or a combination of these.

The Enochian squares

While the Tattvas provided an alternative means to the Tarot for entering 'inner space', they were individual paths of entry, rather than a *series of symbolic states which would lead to the transformation of the magician himself.*

The visions of the so-called Enochian system of magic also allow similar scope, but again the magician ventures inward through an isolated elemental doorway, rather than embarking on a shamanistic journey through a series of archetypes.

Historically the system derives from a series of communications in the trance state involving one Edward Kelley, and Queen Elizabeth I's astrologer, Dr John Dee. Kelley and Dee employed a number of ritual devices in order to contact certain angelic beings in the 'spirit vision'. The angels appeared in a crystal or 'shewstone' and appeared to point with a wand to certain letters which equated in turn with a set of large squares filled with figures of the alphabet, that Dee and Kelley had themselves drawn up. The angels dictated certain powerful 'calls' or conjurations, and these, together with four of the major squares, were used by the magicians of the Golden Dawn as aids for venturing on to the astral planes.

The four major tablets of letters were ascribed to each of the four elements. There was also a smaller fifth tablet containing rows of letters which were interpreted to be the god-names of the elements, for example:

EXARP – Air; HCOMA – Water; NANTA – Earth; BITOM – Fire

A special method of pronunciation was also employed.

The magical method of 'projection' was to select a specific square within the much larger tablet and visualize it three-dimensionally so that it became a truncated pyramid. Each square would have different combinations of elemental and zodiacal influences bearing on it, and the visions produced in the out-of-the-body state were accordingly a complex mix of symbolism. They were made more elaborate again by the Golden Dawn practice of visualizing Egyptian gods surmounting the pyramids. Isis was said to be predominantly a water goddess, Horus, one of fire and Osiris of spirit. Anubis, on the other hand, the well-known guardian of the dead, was a combination of air and earth. Other deities were ascribed up to three elemental 'components'.

One such was Ahephi, one of the children of Horus, and said to embody fire, water and earth. The following record of a Golden Dawn astral encounter demonstrates the principle that the vision is a symbolic resultant of the elements of entry:[4]

> Formed pyramid over me. Went through it . . . and saw Ahephi in the centre of the brilliance, and himself light and white . . . I said I wanted to interview the Sphinx of the pyramid . . . I saw him easily and at once but his colours were not brilliant. I asked him to explain to me the forces to which he corresponded, beginning with the universal force he represented.
>
> *Answer:* I represent active forces acting between the waters above and the waters below the firmament dividing the waters and energized by Fire . . . you may see it in nature in the weather, where the Fire and Air keep the upper and nether waters apart. It represents a cloudy atmosphere with a sea below, but the air between is dry and in active motion; there is no chance of rain, nor is there much evaporation from the surface . . . .

This is not a record of the complete vision, for the magician concerned later had an encounter with a symbolically attired angelic being and surveyed the surroundings from the top of the pyramid. My point in quoting it, however, is that the contents of the vision square closely with the elements ascribed to the doorway of entry.

The occult secrets gained from the supernatural entities, the god, the sphinx and the angel, are hardly profound, and are in a sense quite predictable.

We can regard the Tattvas and the Enochian squares as useful symbols on which to focus the imagination. The symbols come to life in the visionary state as the magician enters the astral plane of the creative psyche. But the point I would like to make here is this: it is not so important that the visions represent embodiments of various elements —

what is far more crucial is what I would like to call 'the span of consciousness' allowed by each symbolic encounter.

A magician concentrating on a symbol of fire meditatively, will produce visionary results of fire, and with earth, results of earth and so on. But such a symbol constitutes a limitation, a confinement of the senses. He is bound by his symbol of entry, for this symbol determines the 'span of consciousness' possible in the circumstances.

The Tattvas and the Enochian squares are thus restricted because in each instance they are individual and unconnected paths of entry into the symbolic realms of the psyche. They do not allow the magician to expand, as it were, once he is in the trance state.

The system of the Major Tarot Arcana is, however, more far-reaching. Here we have a series of pictorial images, which allows the shaman to journey from one inner landscape to another. He grows through the succession of visual encounters and enlarges his domain by virtue of his meeting with the deities of the Tarot pantheon. His span of consciousness is unlimited because the Tree of Life framework is itself open-ended.

Richard Cavendish has written:[5]

> The Golden Dawn's method of meditation on Tarot cards was well calculated to produce the intended effects. The meditator had an idea of the significance of each trump and its path on the Tree to begin with, and he knew the 'correspondences' – the gods, animals, plants, colours and the rest – which expressed its nature . . . .

Cavendish implies in this remark that the Golden Dawn approach was somehow invalid – it pre-empted its own results. It seems to me that we need to consider the Tarot from another angle however. The more familiar the magician is with the Tarot symbolism, the more real it can become imaginatively on the astral plane of the creative imagination. If it then triggers archetypal experiences because of the validity of the symbolism as a sequence of magical images, then the method has proved successful. Clearly the magicians of the Golden Dawn were not finding absolutes inside their heads – they were following, or even imposing, a system of magical images as a particular programme to be followed. What is far more important is the span of consciousness allowed within the programme. There are twenty-two cards of this mythological domain of the Tarot and I will discuss each one in turn, my emphasis being on the Tarot as a growth series rather than isolated symbolic representations.

The shaman who uses the Tarot cards as his doors of entry to the unconscious mind, enters with the card of *The World*. This card, while ostensibly feminine – a dancing maiden within a wreath of corn – is actually latently hermaphroditic, for the figure contains both sexualities.

The shaman traditionally enters through a doorway, a subterranean tunnel, or through a gap in a rock-face, and comes upon the sacred territory which medieval lyricists called faerie-land and which other cultures have called the vault of the heavens or depicted as a journey upon the sacred tree. The Tarot card of *The World* leads out of Malkuth on a direct vertical ascent, and in this sense the magician who takes this path is, in a very real sense, beginning to climb the Qabalistic Tree of Life.

There are two other paths of entry: *Judgment* which leads to the left-hand side of the Tree and the sephirah Hod; and *The Moon* which leads to Netzach. These paths symbolize different aspects of the human temperament. Hod is more the rational, intellectual sphere which mirrors in a lesser form the constructive, uplifting and maintaining role of Thoth/Zeus/Jupiter – the overseer of the heavens. The Hod–Mercury link pertains to the messengers of the gods – an early card in ascending through the pantheon of archetypal energies.

Judgment shows figures holding their arms aloft in tribulation at the call of Gabriel's trumpet. They are reborn, re-awakened to the inner psyche. But the key here is the vibratory mantra, the very essence of being in magical philosophy which actually causes regeneration. We re-awaken according to our capacity to receive.

The Moon like a number of cards, presents a 'triangular' aspect to the sephirah Yesod which it mirrors, that is to say it appears directly opposite Hod as a path. It is a feminine, lunar card, ruled by the moon which watches carefully over the evolutionary aspects presented to view. We see an emerging crustacean, the evolution of the wild wolf into the domestic dog, man's symbols of dominance – the castle and parapets – in the distance. Once again we glimpse the structure of the natural order but the clear direction is towards the sky, the vault of the cosmic order beyond man as he is in the unregenerated state.

Yesod links with the genital regions of microcosmic man and typically indicates the animal, sexual instincts, the region of the inner man called *Nephesch* by the traditional Qabalists.

Two cards lead out of this sphere to each side of the Tree, once again in a 'balancing' divergence – one to Hod and the other to Netzach. One is solar, the other lunar – *The Sun*, and *The Star* respectively.

Again the cards relate to energy sources in the vicinity. *The Sun* to the solar archetype of Tiphareth – again the triangular relationship – and *The Star* to the lunar archetype of Yesod.

Yesod is one of the domains of the White Goddess. We will meet her again in her two roles, the aloof virginal goddess, and the proud and fulfilled Mother of Creation. Diana and Hecate are also aspects of this energy source and *The Star* depicts a beautiful naked maiden kneeling in the waters of spirit, and pouring their life-providing energies onto the earth below. This card mirrors *The Magus* – the virginal magician at the top of the Tree who transmits in like fashion the power of Kether down its entirety. The seven minor stars in the sky seem to focus on the central power source (Kether/the Trinity) and to surround it in the same way that the seven lower spheres on the Tree represent the seven 'days' of Creation.

These cards then, are representative of growth, awakening and emergence. In *The World* and *Judgment* we are reaching into the psyche. *The Star* shows that fruitful intuitive energies flow from an inner, sacred source at a quite early stage of the shaman's journey.

The Sun is similarly transitional. The Sun, resplendent in its golden intensity dominates the top part of the card, but the young children who play in its radiance are not yet fully grown. Shamanistically they are young upon the journey, and we will find them depicted again later in *The Lovers*, where they have matured, and in *The Fool*, where they have fused hermaphroditically beyond sexual division.

We have now completed an early cycle of growth through the Tarot symbols which requires consolidation through the first of the 'horizontal' cards upon the Tree, *The Tower*. We are immediately aware of the relation of this card to the Nephesch for it is especially phallic. But there is a profound lesson incorporated in the card, which is that *The Tower* also symbolizes the human framework. The body of inner man has to be internally balanced and well-structured if it is to withstand the lightning flash from Kether which will strike its turrets destructively unless the shaman is able to transform it. There are hints too of the vanity underlying the Tower of Babel. The shaman must tread warily. His personality will undergo transformation as he journeys higher. But the first lesson is that his pride and his ego must be left behind.

The card which takes the shaman beyond this domain is a card of balance and evolution once again – *Temperance*. On Aleister Crowley's rendition of the card we are shown an angel stirring a cauldron – a universal shamanistic symbol – and fusing therein all the elements of which man is mythologically composed. On Paul Foster Case's version of the same card we see a sun rising between two mountains in the background beyond the archangel of fire – a hint that the god-energy, the Kundalini, is rising in the shaman himself if he can attain it.

Raphael is almost like a guardian; he is awesome and impressive with his vessels of fire. But he protects the worthy and symbolizes strength and inner preserve.

Temperance leads to Tiphareth, which is a vital part of the Tree. We have here the hub of the inner mandala, the centre which mythologically is described as the sun around which the planets of the zodiac rotate – a prime symbol of balance and harmony. It is the first major initiation for the shaman. He emerges from the cauldron of forthcoming as a warrior regenerated by the spirit. He is fortified against the demonic imagery of his lower unconscious and he will be able to proceed now on two quite harrowing paths, *Justice* and *The Hermit*.

It is important to note that Tiphareth is a card of transition rather than an end in itself. Osiris and Christ were both solar gods of transition, bridging a gap between man and the very source of creation. The mystic seeks to enter that undifferentiated source of being which has been variously described as *sartori*, *nirvana* and cosmic consciousness, a domain in which the individual and the universal have become One, and Tiphareth points the way to this exalted state.

Two dramatic cards adjoining Tiphareth show that one of the great shamanistic myths unfolded at this stage is the death/renewal process. We find here *Death* (Netzach–Tiphareth) and *The Devil* (Hod–Tiphareth), both of which show in different ways man coming to grips with his 'lower' nature. On *Death* an angry skeletal figure wields a scythe above a crop of human heads and broken bodies. But we notice that beyond the field of carnage a river flows into the sun, and it is clear that Death removes the limiting and unwanted aspects of the human personality – pride and arrogance and so on – and like *Temperance* exerts a restructuring effect. *The Devil* is the last attempt of the psyche to exert a sense of ego in the animal domain. The Devil sits triumphant over a man and woman whose bestial aspects are crudely shown by horns, tails and cloven hoofs. They stand shackled to his throne . . . a reminder that they are trapped by their desires and immediate passions.

The Devil is however a blind; he is the negative face of Tiphareth which can trap the shaman not prepared to journey further. In the sense that Lucifer–Satan was a fallen god he is also a transitional figure, and his kingdom serves as an outer court to the domain of the inner sun.

Justice and *The Hermit* further fortify the shaman on his journey. *Justice* demands brutal self-assessment. We find the polar opposite, the loving and enticing Venus here, for now she holds a threatening sword ready at any moment to cut away self-deception, arrogance and falsehood. The lunar cusp on the sword indicates that she *is* the White Goddess in yet another guise, and she too represents transition; beyond her domain and shielded by a veil, is the land of the great gods of the higher regions on the Tree.

The Hermit depicts what various mystical traditions have called the Dark Night of the Soul. The Hermit trusts to his inner voice for guidance but he travels alone upon the dark, icy slopes of the cosmic mountain. His ego is diminished now; he wears the robes of anonymity and is beginning to awaken to the wisdom of The Ancient of Days (Chesed) in whose direction he climbs.

If *The Hermit* and *Justice* are both powerful cards of rigorous self-evaluation *The Wheel of Fortune* and *The Hanged Man* are cards of encouragement. *The Wheel*, which again mirrors the mandala-like effect that Tiphareth exerts in the centre of the Tree depicts a universal vortex of life energies. On the other side of the Tree meanwhile, we find *The Hanged Man*, who in a very appropriate way, is more clearly thought of, not as a murdered villain, but as a reflection of a higher principle. Much has been made of the symbolism of what purports to be a crude sacrifice on a wooden edifice. *The Hanged Man*, like *The Wheel of Fortune* does of course mirror the death-renewal or resurrection-rebirth concepts which are integral parts of the Tiphareth energy vortex and crucial to all solar myths including those of Apollo, Dionysus, Osiris and Christ.

The Hanged Man, who is best depicted mythologically in the Thoth pack of Aleister Crowley, reflects the watery domains of the great ocean of spirit (Maris — the virgin sea, the great Mother of form) and as such is a beacon to the world below — a very appropriate mythological function which the historical Christ performed in the world during his incarnation.

We come to the second horizontal card upon the Tree at this stage: *Strength*. It is interesting that, whereas the traditional Qabalah is very much dominated by the different faces of the great male archetype, the Tarot card which unites Geburah (Strength) and Chesed (Mercy) is one depicting the Great Mother. Feminine intuition and grace dominate an angry lion, symbolic of the final victory of higher thought over the animal instincts inherent in lower man.

It is at this stage that we have really begun to pass beyond the animal kingdom – man's traditional domain – altogether. The final cards are renditions of very powerful inner spaces, awesome energies which owe far more to the basic spirit of the cosmos than to man's individual perceptions.

In a shamanistic sense, the remaining Tarot cards really attempt to depict a transcendental process almost beyond imagery. However, the magical shaman requires milestones on the sacred inner territory and these cards are, in this capacity, an inner structuring of his journey, which takes him through the vault of the heavens and wards off the Qlippothic elements of chaos which are present at all stages on the Tree of Life.[6]

As mentioned earlier, *The Lovers* depicts a more evolved form of the energy level represented by *The Sun*. On *The Lovers* we see the young maiden and her youthful escort moving towards a state of inner union. Love produces a state of balance and, more importantly, *totality*; the sense of transcendental completeness which is of course appropriate to Kether – the sourcepoint of all creation. Love in itself is very much an attribute of the Great Mother (Binah – *The Empress*) who gave birth to them, and the card is a journeying home towards the Source.

The love of the divine son and the divine maiden (Tiphareth and Malkuth) is mirrored on yet a more exalted level by the polar contrasts of *The Empress* and *The Emperor*. These are the great archetypes overviewing creation and take the function in the universe called the demiurge, the maintainer and overseer of what has in itself emanated from a more subtle, unformulated level.

If we regard the living universe as a source of energy forms, some of which are manifest in growing organisms and others resident in forms which have outlived their usefulness, it is clear that any mythological set must depict the polarity of growth and destruction. We find the merciful, maintaining role in the card of *The Emperor* especially. He is Zeus and Jupiter, the great father archetype who watches benignly upon his domain and subjects below. But his other face is destructive and in the Tarot it is represented by *The Charioteer* who unlike the stable, stationary Emperor seated on his stone throne, moves actively and vengefully through the universe of form. He is the warrior (Geburah – Mars) whose purpose it is to destroy and eliminate growth forms which are themselves impeding the evolutionary process.

51

The Charioteer mirrors the energy of the Great Mother/Ocean of Being in the sense that he is a warrior of water (he bears a crab as an emblem on his helmet) and also holds as his weapon, not a sword, but a mirror – for he is the all-seeing eye. Once again, the Crowley Thoth cards depict this process most accurately. The more familiar Waite– Case packs by contrast lack the vital sense of motion and activity which distinguishes this card from the more passive symbolism of *The Emperor*.

The Hierophant, which like *The Emperor* is aligned to Chokmah, is similarly a face of The Ancient of Days, the arbiter of spiritual wisdom in the universe. But he also represents a principle that, church institutions in the present day occasionally forget, namely that spiritual authority derives from inner experience. In this sense a priest or church father should hold his post because of his ability to transmit inner knowledge to his congregation.

The occult revival and the diminishing of Christian influence in particular is no doubt related to a human craving for archetypal recognition – we all need the mystical experiences of inner certainty. The contemporary prevalence of gurus indicates a widespread need for people to follow those who claim to embody in different ways the inner light. *The Hierophant* incorporates in its design the somewhat heretical suggestion that the Pope should also be a mystic – a prospect that historical Christianity has not condoned.

The three remaining cards of the Tarot-shaman's pantheon of images are *The High Priestess*, *The Magus* and *The Fool*. If we bear in mind that one mythological means of representing a pure state of being is by depicting the archetype as virginal (totally beyond blemish, a symbol of transcendence) then *The High Priestess* and *The Magus* are the virginal equivalent forms of *The Empress* and *The Emperor* who 'know' each other by virtue of their bringing forth the offspring of creation.

The High Priestess sits beyond a veil of mist, an ethereal distant rendition of the White Goddess who, in a lower form, was more active in the world of images. But *The High Priestess* is totally withdrawn – her domain extends vertically on the upper half of the Tree of Life, beyond the Abyss which cleaves the Tree into essence and form. In the symbol of *The High Priestess* we have a transcendental and almost unknowable form of the White Goddess.

Similarly in *The Magus*, we find a male archetype who is already subject to the androgynous aspects inherent in Kether. He is not masculine in the sense that *The Charioteer* or *The Emperor* are. His face is soft and feminine, and although his act of transmitting magical inspiration down the causeways of the Tree is an act of power, his authority is inherent rather than felt. His symbols are clear – he manipulates the wand and sword of masculinity, and the cup and pentacle of femininity, which will later become forceful motifs in the creative imagination. But he is hardly a figure in the world of actuality; he too is transcendent.

Finally, *The Fool* depicts a most precarious state of being. *The Fool* is a young virginal person whose sexuality is deliberately unclear, and who hovers between the manifest universe and the Void beyond Form. The shaman at this stage undertakes the final journey. The card invites him to pass beyond form into the undifferentiated state of universal bliss, the infinite and ineffable state of unity and mystery described by the traditional Qabalists as *Ain Soph Aur*, the limitless light.

It is evident that the Major Arcana of the Tarot hardly belong with the other fifty-six minor cards at all. Mythologically they represent a growth process thematically absent from the 'lower' cards, which depict the elemental division into fire, earth, water and air and all its permutations.

While traditional scholarship has rejected the recent suggestion that the Qabalah and Tarot are mutually reinforcing, there is no doubt that quite aside from historical considerations of origin, the two systems together form a very effective shamanistic programme. We discover in the cards, as we enter at the level of earth consciousness, that the shamanistic flight of ecstasy potentially traverses the entire inner universe of the creative imagination.

The Tarot cards are used specifically as a basis of visualization, and the required method is to become sufficiently acquainted with the symbolism of each card so that it can be imagined in full detail at the dictate of the will. The magician thus conjures it into appearance as part of a sequence of symbolic locations which define his venture into inner space. The venture may be undertaken meditatively but it is far more 'real' when combined with the out-of-the-body experience.

Three Tarot packs are commonly available which owe their formulation to the Golden Dawn and allied systems of magic and we have referred to them already. These are the Rider pack designed by A. E. Waite and Pamela Coleman Smith; the BOTA pack of Paul Foster Case and Jessie Burns Parke and the Thoth pack of Aleister Crowley, illustrated by Lady Frieda Harris.

The first two of these are relatively traditional and portray the symbols of each card in a decorative rather than an experimental way.

53

The Thoth pack however is designed very much to portray the actual magical reality and symbolic domain of each card, and as a set they are much more a part of the tradition of visionary art than any other existing pack. We need to remember, however, that they are also tinged by Crowley's own personal magical world-view, and certain aberrations are present in their format. After his sojourn in Egypt, Crowley actively switched his allegiance from ceremonial to sexual magic and from this time onwards defined his shamanistic identity in terms of the Egyptian pantheon of gods and a somewhat garbled rendition of the anti-Christ account found in *The Book of Revelation*. For example we find *Strength*, which normally depicts a maiden overcoming the brute strength of a lion, replaced instead by *Lust*, and showing a rather indulgent scarlet lady, the Whore of Babalon, revelling on the back of a multi-headed, atavistic chimera.

Nevertheless, in a visual sense Crowley's pack is our basic point of commencement for the shamanistic tradition in the West. The following meditative descriptions are built on the basic symbolic content of each card and offer a visual summary of each doorway. Accompanying each description is what I have called a 'technique of passage' – a means of confronting the mythological imagery and responding to it.

The World

A naked maiden dances joyfully in a wreath of wheat. She also holds two wands, one in each hand, and the Hebrew letter Tau, meaning salvation, swirls around her body like a mantle. At the four corners of this symbolic entry through the earth are the four apocalyptic creatures of *The Book of Revelations*: man, bull, lion and eagle.

Technique of passage: The wreath of wheat defines the outer limits of a tunnel or vortex through which the shaman will enter. Regard the dance of the maiden as symbolic of the interplay of creative energies in all creation.

Judgment

The angel Gabriel, with golden hair and a dazzling blue robe holds forth a long stemmed trumpet, and its resonant, melodious sound causes seemingly dead figures to arise from graves with their hands uplifted. The coffins surprisingly float on water and this sea is really the ocean of spirit of the Great Mother. A banner depicting a red cross on a white field, symbolic of rebirth, is attached to the neck of the trumpet.

Technique of passage: Rise up on the waves of sound, identifying with the vigour of rebirth which the trumpet proclaims.

The Sun

Two young and innocent children dance at the foot of a grassy hill. A brick wall separates the children from its peak while a radiant, golden sun fills the sky with its brilliance. Sunflowers growing on the wall entice the children to grow toward the light.

Technique of passage: Enjoy the recovered sense of innocence with your young partner of the opposite sex. Feel the waves of sunlight reaching down, playing on the skin, yet drawing you into the energy vortex which is the sun itself. Respect the sanctity of the domain beyond the wall for it is a sacred place.

The Moon

The lunar crescent dominates the sky and sends down showers of silvery light particles upon the kingdom below. Two dogs, one wild and the other tame howl at the sky; a lobster struggles out of the water onto the bank, battling against the limitations of its form. Man's castle turrets, grey and built of heavy stone, reach up to the sky as a symbol of his dominance of nature.

Technique of passage: Reflect on the evolutionary processes that you see before you – the struggle of the lobster to evolve into a land-form shape, the metamorphosis of the wild, brutish dog into a more refined domestic creature, the place of man in the natural domain. Regard the silvery moon-pellets as a dew, a subtle life essence which fertilizes and makes more complete the dominating energy of the sun.

The Star

A beautiful naked maiden reaches up to the sky with a silver goblet and captures the fructifying essences of a night-star. These flow through her as if she were a translucent, glass vessel and well up into a cup she holds in her other hand. She empties the life-giving fluids onto barren earth. The landscape is resplendent in a pearly grey and mauve half-light. When the maiden moves, the atmosphere seems to shimmer like liquid silver.

Technique of passage: Enjoy the sensation of entering into the process of the transmission of spirit and life-force from one vessel to the other. Re-live the process of subtle essence manifesting in an earthen context.

The Tower

A fierce bolt of lightning strikes and crumbles the stone battlements of a lofty tower. Chunks of masonry, a golden crown which surmounted the tower, and two unfortunate human beings, hurtle earthwards. The sky is ablaze with violent, all-subsuming red and orange flame and a vengeful eye can be seen in the centre of the angry heavens, surveying the vanity of man in trying to build a tower to reach skywards.

Technique of passage: Feel the electric discharge in the air and endeavour to identify with the ruined tower while imagining that at the same time it enlarges itself into a more strongly fortified dwelling, capable of withstanding the wrath of the lightning bolt. Regard your body as a tower which has to be built on sound foundations with no inner conflicts of intent. The tower itself is now raised anew with humility and respect for the energy sources which sustain the universe.

The Devil

Two degraded human beings with horns and tails stand chained to a stone pedestal on which perches the grotesque form of the horned Devil. He has eagle's claws and bat's wings, and a goat's head surmounted by an inverted white pentagram. His body is flashy and coloured earthen brown and the presence of a breast suggests that he is in some degree hermaphroditic. He holds a torch downwards in his left hand and his right is held open as if in mock salute.

Technique of passage: Encounter the Devil but reflect on his incongruous nature; he is an absurd idol of worship which makes all the more tragic the plight of other human beings chained to his command. Dwell on the imagery of the devil's face and, realizing that it is a mask which conceals a greater inner reality beyond its outward pretences, feel yourself passing through the hollow cavities of the eyes.

Death

A frenzied skeleton wielding a scythe dances insanely through a field of human heads. Scattered carnage litters the ground but the spirits of the dead merge and flow into a river which wends its way through a valley into the land of the inner sun. The skeleton is an ashen grey colour, the sky is flaccid like a heavy, pervasive liquid suggestive of astral forms.

Technique of passage: Allow your body to be hewn to pieces, identifying at the same time with the greater, spiritual personality which is released from bondage, and which will now flow with the tides of the spirit. Regard 'death', at this stage, as a process of refinement.

Temperance

A golden headed angelic being with enormous outstretched, shimmering wings stands in the stream of Life with one foot on the ground, and one in water. His gown is pure white and a radiant golden disk shines from his forehead. Above him a beautiful rainbow spans the sky.

In his right hand he holds a flask, and he pours water from it onto the head of a scowling dusky lion who lies subdued near his right foot. In his other hand he holds a blazing torch, whose flames shower onto the head of a silver eagle.

Beyond the angel a sun can be seen rising between two mountain peaks and the stream is seen to flow down from this more elevated source.

Technique of passage: Regard the angel as a spiritual being who provides a profound sense of inner balance. He represents the fusion of the elements into a state of harmony and the stability he offers is a requirement of entry into Tiphareth, the sphere of the sun which lies just beyond the mountain peaks.

The Hanged Man

A young man wearing red tights and a blue jacket whose pockets bear emblems of the moon, hangs upside down from a wooden gallows.

The gallows are in the form of the Hebrew letter Tau and he is attached by his right leg, with a rope, to the cross-beam above. His hands are clasped behind his back out of vision but make a triangular shape with his body. His left leg meanwhile is bent, forming a cross with his suspended right leg. The focal point of attention however is the man's head which shines like a beacon, emitting an illuminating radiance. The atmosphere is watery as if, in one sense, the hanged man is a reflection in a rippling pool rather than inverted in his own right.

Technique of passage: Imagine yourself drawing near to the beacon which is the hanged man's head and then merge with it so that you begin to reflect the light which he is transmitting from above. Reflect on the sacrifice which the subtle inner light has to make in penetrating denser matter and inwardly thank the figure of the hanged man for acting as an intermediary between matter and spirit.

The Wheel of Fortune

The giant cosmic wheel, the pivot of the manifested universe, turns on its axis amid tides of energy which disperse to all corners of the universe. The ten-spoked wheel is golden in colour and is surmounted by a vigilant sphinx bearing a sword who remains stationary at the crest of the wheel as it turns purposefully beneath him. A yellow serpent coils itself around the left hand side of the wheel and the Egyptian jackal-headed god resides on the right hand. Once again the four creatures of *Revelations* – man, eagle, bull and lion – are present in the four quarters – all golden in colour against a blue sky.

Technique of passage: The Wheel of Fortune is itself a mandala, a symbol of infinity. Concentrate on the centre-point, the focus of the eternal process of unfoldenment: and pass through it regarding it once again as a symbol of transformation.

The Hermit

A bearded sage stands holding a lantern in which shines a six-pointed golden star. He carries a staff in his other hand and wears a full-length cloak of dark grey. Gradually he traverses the rocky, icy path on the side of the mystical mountain of created being. He is a lone traveller, very much guided by the illumination of his lantern.

Technique of passage: This card teaches us to trust the guiding inspiration of the inner self, the Holy Guardian Angel. Reflect on the anonymous quality of the sage's appearance, the absence of outwardly expressed individuality. Identify the lantern as an image of the self and become more firmly resolute in the upward climb to the peak of creation, where individuality will become increasingly less important.

Justice

The White Goddess of Justice sits enthroned in a temple radiant with silver and blue light. In her left hand she holds the scales in which she will weigh the spiritual qualities of all who come before her. Her two-edged sword, with a hilt consisting of lunar crescents is a symbol of impeccable authority. Her hair is golden, her robe red and her cape green. She is the warlike aspect of Venus, and guardian of the sacred territory of golden light which lies beyond the confines of her temple.

Technique of passage: Following the process of refinement and self-transformation that we found in *Death*, allow yourself to be judged impartially by *Justice* and submit to her trials. Realize that it is in fact the loving side of the higher self that sits in judgment and that only illusions and inconsistencies will be ruthlessly disbanded.

Strength

A woman with a wreath of coloured flowers in her hair stands silhouetted against a yellow sky, restraining the anger of a red lion. Her cloak is pure white and she wears red roses around her waist. The lion is clearly subservient to her for she places roses around its neck too.

Technique of passage: Identify with the forces of intuition and patience inherent in controlling the animal instincts which are at the core of all human activity. Become the woman of the flowers and take her place holding in check the primal energies of the lower self.

The Charioteer

A warrior with golden armour, his helmet bearing the insignia of the crab and his elbows adorned with lunar crescents, rides in a chariot drawn by two sphinxes, one black and the other white. The roof of his chariot is vivid blue flecked with stars and the wheels and body of his carriage a warlike red. He holds in his hands a mirror in which he sees, in the manner of an all-perceiving eye, the unwanted aspects of creation which are ripe for destruction.

Technique of passage: Assume the role of the warrior and imagine the mirror reflecting inwardly on yourself, in an act of rigid self-scrutiny. Enter into the sense of flux which is the process of life and death itself, and regard the warrior not so much as a wanton destroyer but as a scourge of unconstructive and conflicting elements which stand in the way of inner unity.

The Lovers

An angel wearing a violet robe and with arms outstretched sanctifies the two lovers, who stand naked in a state of innocence regained. Behind Eve is the Tree of the Knowledge of Good and Evil bearing five fruits; a serpent coils around its trunk. Behind Adam resides another tree whose fruits are twelve flames each with three tongues representative of the signs of the Zodiac. A golden sun illuminates the sky above the angel and in the distance of the far horizon we see the mystical mountain showing its peak.

Technique of passage: This card represents the fusion of sexual polarities in the self, a further transformation towards union beyond duality. Consequently the basic impact of this symbolism is recognizing and fusing lovingly with the complementary sexual polarity, embracing the other aspect of one's masculine or feminine nature.

The Hierophant

The High Priest sits on a grey throne fashioned from stone. His robe is red, edged in green, his blue undergarment visible as he raises his hands. He wears a triple-layered golden crown and holds in his left hand a golden staff with three cross-bars near the top. His right hand is uplifted, bestowing blessings. His shoes are white and are inscribed with crosses, and near by, lying crossed on a red carpet, are two keys; one silver (lunar) and the other golden (solar).

Technique of passage: The Hierophant embodies spiritual authority but simultaneously bestows grace on those who have ears to hear. Again he represents the gradual fusion of solar and lunar principles.

The Emperor

The Emperor sits on his throne carved from a cubic stone, surveying the kingdom of manifest creation. He holds in his right hand a wand surmounted by the head of Aries the ram, and the same motif appears on his armour. In his left hand he holds a globe surmounted by a cross, and he is seated with his left leg crossed over his right, the cross in both instances symbolizing the figure four (Chesed: Mercy – the fourth sephirah). Except for his white beard, the vision of the Emperor is dominated by the colour red, the colour of Mars, which rules Aries. The Emperor is facing towards the left and we see only his profile: he is a form of the Ancient of Days.

Technique of passage: The Emperor, although a merciful aspect of the Great Father archetype, is approached with respect. He should nevertheless be regarded as in some ways unfulfilled – his kingdom is barren without the *Empress*, and he owes as much to her as *The Hanged Man*, who similarly had his legs crossed in the sign of four, and also reflected the Great Ocean. The shaman passes from the rocky, mountainous kingdom of the Emperor to the more welcome and abundant pastures of the Empress.

The Empress

The Empress is the Great Mother of Creation. She sits on a throne in a fleld of wheat, a row of cypresses in the background. Her robe and dress are russet and green, colours of the earth, and her hair flows down her shoulders in long golden swirls. In her right hand she bears a heart-shaped shield inscribed with a dove, and in her left, a sceptre bearing a globe surmounted by a cross. A silver crescent is visible beneath her foot and twelve silver stars shine around her forehead. Near by the river of life pours down upon the crops providing irrigation for a fruitful harvest.

Technique of passage: The Empress is the supreme representation of Mother Nature, the great womb of all manifested forms, and to encounter her is to return to the very source of created being. It is a reaffirmation of the process of life and fulfilment itself, the home of the river of life. The shaman surrenders himself to the source of his form.

The High Priestess

The High Priestess sits on a stone throne beyond a sheen of silver mist. She wears a lunar crown and a shimmering blue cloak which falls in folds suggestive of water, to the temple floor. In her hand she holds the scroll of memory, and on her breast she wears an equal-armed cross. Her manner is cold and aloof; she is the supreme virgin goddess. On her right side stands a black column and on her left a white one. Between these is a veil which renders invisible the sacred territory beyond creation.

Technique of passage: The shaman here enters sublime, virginal ground — the very essence of the universe before its fall into form. This region is the first symbolic domain which will take him undifferentiated into the void of the space.

The Magus

The Magician holds his wand aloft, receiving the energy of the prime creative impulse, and with his left hand points downwards towards the direction of the manifest universe. He is the supreme transmitter of energy but resides, himself, above form. His cloak is red, his bodice pure white. Around his waist is a coiled snake swallowing its tail. The Magus has before him the four symbols which are the language of creation: the cup, the pentacle, the sword and the wand. His domain is filled with golden-white brilliance.

Technique of passage: The magus is the male virgin who has not had contact with the female polarity in order to reproduce and bring about form. He is pure energy and like the High Priestess remains transcendental and essentially unknowable.

The Fool

The Fool represents the supreme mystery. He is depicted as a youth — perhaps male, perhaps female, about to step over a cliff into the void. The Fool's outer garment is floral and multi-coloured, incorporating numerous solar mandala motifs and a single silver star. The inner garment is a pure dazzling white.

The expression on the face of the heavenly androgyne is one of high indifference – the balance between force and form, between male and female, being fine and precarious.

Technique of passage: Within the shaman's journey, this is the supreme path, in which the magician dissolves his very being in the void of the final mystery.

We have considered at length the shamanistic implications of the Tarot as a series of inner visions. The god-energies which they lead to in the psyche are vortexes of considerable authority and creative impact. They are such that they transform the shaman on his journey.

However we should consider not only the 'span of consciousness' opened by the Tarot but also the reasons for its internal balance, the harmony resident in its very structure when superimposed on the Tree of Life.

The god levels

We have described the gods as symbolic representations of energy states. They depict the forceful interaction of the intellect, intuition and emotions, and they characterize our instincts and passions.

David Miller in his *The New Polytheism* writes:[7]

We are the playground of a veritable theatre full of Gods and Goddesses. What do the Gods and Goddesses want with us? Our task is to incarnate them, become aware of their presence, acknowledge and celebrate their forms so that we may better be able to account for our polytheism.

The Qabalistic levels are tenfold and reflect the traditional Judaic patriarchal consciousness although the addition of Tarot symbolism in the modern context has, significantly, restored the balance of polarities.

The Ten Sephiroth are:

Kether
Chokmah
Binah
Chesed
Geburah

Tiphareth
Netzach
Hod
Yesod
Malkuth

In the traditional mythological sense these levels on the Tree are:

Neutral
Male
Female
Male
Male
Male/Neutral
Female
Male
Female
Female/Neutral

There are several methods for testing the internal balance of the Tree of Life and the Major Tarot Arcana. From the mythological viewpoint the Tree appears as in Figure 2.

Method 1: Polarities at levels

Binah and Chokmah are polarities of feminine and masculine, but both emanate from the Void of Space, Ain Soph Aur, which resides above duality. The alchemists depicted this state by means of a symbol of a king and queen joined together.

Binah and Chokmah represent the first division into form and force; the second division into a major polarity occurs at the next level between Geburah and Chesed where masculine aspects represent, once again, force and form.

At the next stage of descent Tiphareth is the masculine product of the union of the Great Father and the Great (virginal) Mother of Heaven. Tiphareth is in the centre of the Tree like the focus of a wheel, the centre of a mandala, and is appropriately represented by the sun. The sun gives life and accordingly is masculine (force aspect) but its position is on the 'middle pillar' which provides a tendency towards neutrality. It is interesting that most depictions of the mythological Christ – as one example of the divine son, – show a very feminine and not all aggressive form of masculinity in which internal polarities are resolved.

64

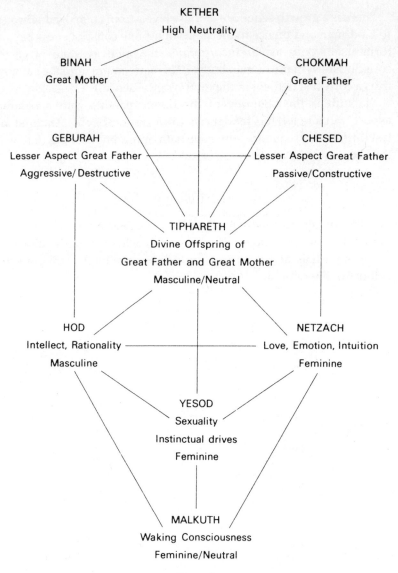

Figure 2

At the next level Hod and Netzach balance as polarities of attitude, one an attitude towards the objective, the definite and the measurable, the other a tendency towards the subjective, the intangible and the emotive.

Yesod as shown by its position on the Tree, resides over the genital region. It is the sphere of all the sexual drives of man.

There is a growth sequence in these levels from animal man through to God-man and thence to the states of infinite consciousness beyond form itself. Any avatar incorporates the midway state of cosmic consciousness in the human body. ('No man cometh unto the Father' is thus a correct statement in the mythological sense.)

Malkuth is the offspring of the divine parents with a feminine aspect, but she too has tendencies towards androgyny. The first and last cards of our sequence both have hermaphroditic qualities, following the occult axiom: 'as above, so below'.

Method 2: Colour polarities

The Tree of Life consists of ten levels of consciousness. These however, can be divided mythologically into the white light of the 'Trinity' – the three supernals at the top of the Tree – combined with the seven colours of the rainbow.

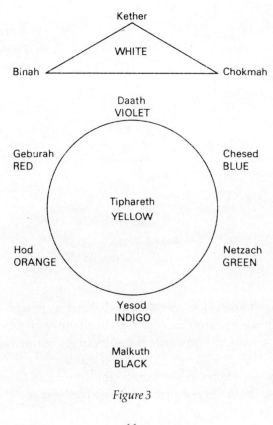

Figure 3

In so doing we separate Malkuth, the state of earth-consciousness from the Tree (which, in the system of chakras, is black in contrast with the white light from the top of the Tree) and we introduce the so-called 'eleventh sephirah', Daath. 'Daath' means knowledge and is ascribed to the Tree midway between Kether and Tiphareth. The Tree of inner man now appears as in Figure 3.

Viewed in this way, the Tree of Life which usually looks especially linear, acquires the property of a mandala containing all the qualities of the rainbow. The shaman who integrates its qualities within his being will indeed have acquired all the attributes of white light. The wheel of inner colours meanwhile is exquisitely poised between light and dark and the growth of consciousness is reminiscent of the ancient Gnostic concept of escaping from darkness to light.

The magicians of the Golden Dawn, as with exponents of yoga, ascribe the energy levels of the Tree to what in the East are called the 'chakras' of inner man.[8]

The chakra-equivalents in magic follow the pattern of the diagram, so that the colours visualized by the magician who is endeavouring to 'bring down the light' of Ain Soph Aur into his own being follow the pattern from Kether down to Malkuth:

White – Violet – Yellow – Indigo – Black.

Meanwhile from the viewpoint, yet again, of internal balance, the remaining colours form two sets of complementaries in a cross upon the Tree:

Red – Green

Orange – Blue

Method 3: The 'dominant' Major Arcana on the Tree of Life

We observe an interesting effect in terms of polarity when we analyse the Tarot ascriptions upon the Tree in terms of what I would like to call 'dominant' cards.

It is clear that several of the Major Tarot Trumps reflect quite directly the symbolism of the sephirah which lies opposite on the Tree in a 'triangular' relationship. For example, both *The Hanged Man*, who is 'crucified' and also shines as a beacon to the world, and also *The Wheel of Fortune*, each show different aspects of Tiphareth. On the one hand *The Hanged Man* is an archetypal variant on the sacrificial saviour, the reborn solar gods like Osiris and Christ, while *The Wheel of Fortune* is a mandala which reflects Tiphareth's position in the centre of the

Zodiacal Tree. Other examples of this 'triangular' situation, in which the card reflects the meaning of the sephirah, are *The Sun, The Moon, The Lovers, Justice* and *The Tower*. Several other cards, notably *The World, The Star, The Hermit, The Charioteer, The Hierophant* and *The Fool* very strongly reflect the sephirah they are *linked* to.

Quite apart from this consideration however, it is possible to take each of the ten sephiroth, and to isolate 'triads' of Tarot cards which lead out each of those sephiroth in an evolutionary direction. It is necessary to stress that we are considering the symbolism only of those cards which represent *growth upwards*, for this reflects the true shamanistic purpose. (Several sephiroth on the Tree, of course, have triads which reach downwards.)

The pattern of triads which emerges can be shown as follows:

MALKUTH	World – Star – Moon (Right-hand side)
	Judgment – Sun – World (Left-hand side)
YESOD	Temperance – Death – Star (Right)
	Sun – Devil – Temperance (Left)
HOD	Devil – Death – Tower (Right)
	Hanged Man – Justice – Devil (Left)
NETZACH	Tower – Devil – Death (Right)
	Death – Hermit – Wheel (Left)
TIPHARETH	High Priestess – Fool – Emperor (High right)
	Emperor – Hierophant – Hermit (Lower right)
	Lovers – Magus – High Priestess (High left)
	Justice – Chariot – Lovers (Lower left)
	Lovers – Empress – Emperor (High centre)
	Justice – Strength – Hermit (Lower centre)
GEBURAH	
CHESED	No evolutionary triads
BINAH	
CHOKMAH	Identical triad:
	Magus – Fool – Empress/Empress – Magus – Fool
KETHER	Upwards beyond the Tree, a triangle whose invisible sides are infinite!

What I will call the 'dominant' Major Tarot cards in this arrangement are those Arcana which occur in both couplets (in the case of Tiphareth due to its position on the Tree we have three pairs of couplets).

The dominants which now emerge are: World – Temperance – Devil – Death – Lovers – High Priestess – Emperor – Empress – Magus –

Fool, that is a total of ten, the number of sephiroth upon the Tree. But more significantly, when evaluating the Tarot as a programme for inner space, the 'dominant' cards are perfectly balanced in terms of structural polarity.

On the Tree the 'dominants' align as follows:

	Fool
Higher Tree	Magus
	Empress
	Emperor
Middle Tree	High Priestess
	Lovers
	Death
	Devil
Lower Tree	Temperance
	World

The polarities of these dominant tarot cards can in some instances be identified as masculine or feminine quite easily. Several of the cards, however, exhibit a fusion of the sexes – *The Fool*, *The Devil* and *The World* all depict androgynous creatures, and *The Lovers* shows the gradual fusion of sexual opposites. Other cards depict a different sort of neutrality; *Temperance* combines all the elements in a balanced totality and *Death*, which depicts a skeleton is necessarily sexless!

We are now in a position to assign a polarity:

	Fool	Neutral
Higher Tree	Magus	Masculine
	Empress	Feminine
	Emperor	Masculine
Middle Tree	High Priestess	Feminine
	Lovers	Neutral
	Death	Neutral
	Devil	Neutral
Lower Tree	Temperance	Neutral
	World	Neutral

This procedure of identifying the dominant cards demonstrates a vital point in assessing the Tarot as a shamanistic method, namely that its structure is internally consistent. We find that the Tarot ascriptions have in a sense re-balanced the heavy patriarchal tendency which was to be found in the traditional Qabalah. Even these cards which exhibit a definite mythological polarity balance beautifully: we have the virginal male and virginal female (*The Magus* and *The High Priestess*) counter-posed by the Great Father and the Great Mother, whose union produces the universe (*The Emperor* and *The Empress*). From the shamanistic viewpoint the pantheon of supernatural beings reflects an ordered universe. The programme, in John Lilly's sense, is a balanced one.

From the equally important viewpoint of colour, the shaman, as with the Jivaro Indian who journeys to the gods in the land of coloured mists, here literally finds himself confronted with a rainbow circle whose totality is white light. His journey takes him through all the colours of the cosmic mandala.

Detail from *Kampf der vervandelten Gotter* (Ernst Fuchs)

Child and Signs in the Sky (Wilfried Satty)

The Haunted Palace (Wilfried Satty)

The Virgin Land (Wilfried Satty)

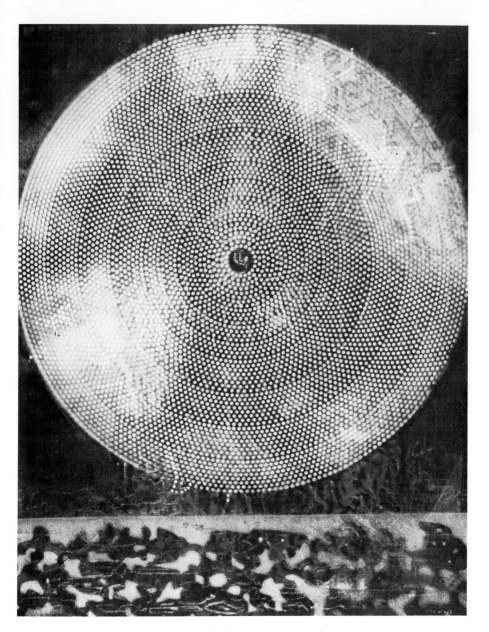

Birth of the Galaxy (Max Ernst)

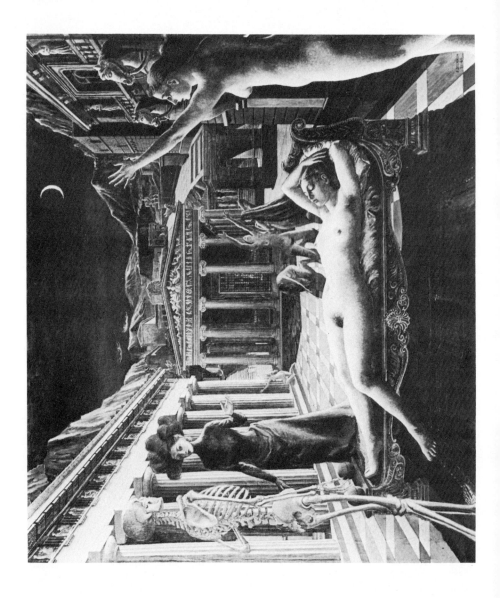

Detail from
Sleeping Venus (Paul Delvaux)

Beliar (Wilfredo Lam)

Santiago El Grande (Salvador Dali)

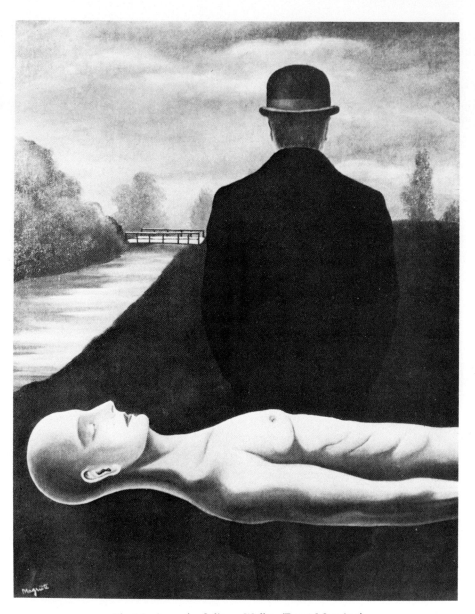

The Musings of a Solitary Walker (René Magritte)

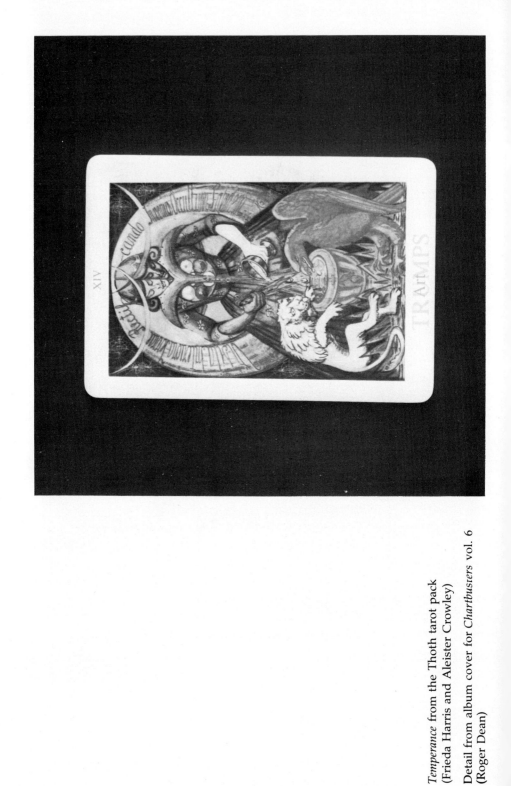

Temperance from the Thoth tarot pack
(Frieda Harris and Aleister Crowley)

Detail from album cover for *Chartbusters* vol. 6
(Roger Dean)

Published by Big O Posters Ltd 219 Eversleigh Road

Album cover for *Relayer* (Roger Dean)

Farewell to Synthesis (Austin Osman Spare)

Jacket cover for *The Bull and the Spear* (Patrick Woodroffe)

What am I doing with my life? (Abdul Mati Klarwein)

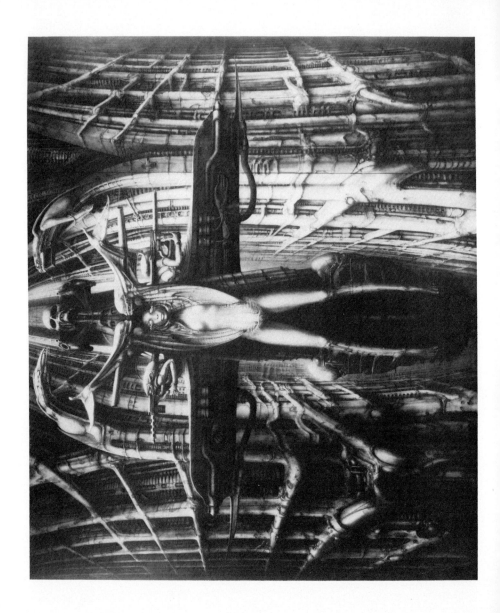

The Spell part I (H. R. Giger)

The Spell part II (H. R. Giger)

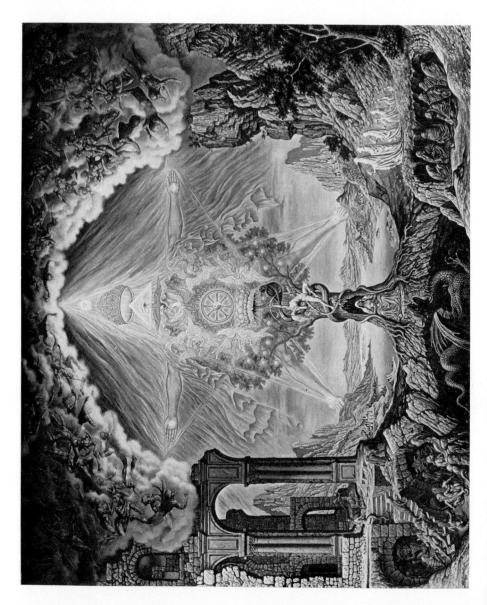

Central panel of
Unio Mystica (Johfra Bosschart)

Rex et Regina II (Diana Vandenberg)

Libra (Johfra Bosschart)

Gemini (Johfra Bosschart)

Individuation (Rosaleen Norton)

Panic (Rosaleen Norton)

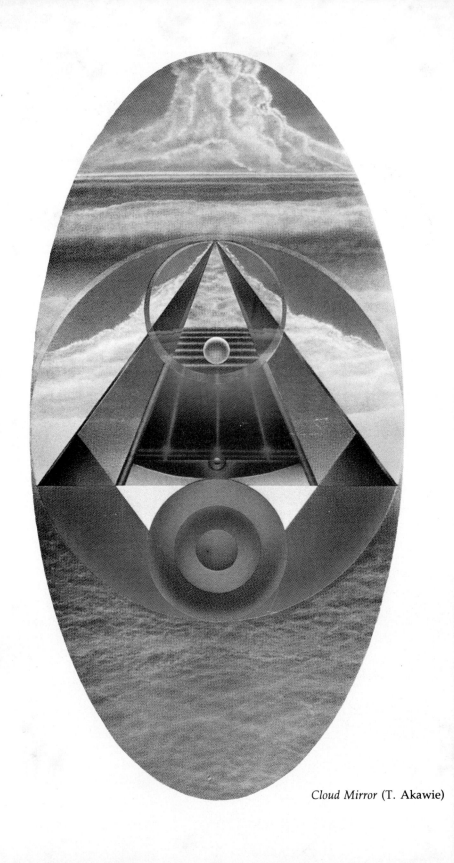

Cloud Mirror (T. Akawie)

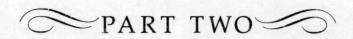

PART TWO

Sound and symbol

Dreams control our reality and the
supreme reality is creativity . . . .

Klaus Schulze
visionary musician

Ecstasy is my frame of reference.

Abdul Mati Klarwein
visionary artist

Surrealism and the Qabalah

Mythology has often interwoven itself with art but never with such variety as in the art of the surrealists. Surrealism and Dadaism constituted an early attempt by a notable group of visionaries to extend reality beyond its confines. André Breton sought in automatic writing and spontaneous art a means of overcoming the meddling interference of the intellect, a direct route into the creative unconscious – a fusion of dream and reality.

It is not surprising that many of the surrealists, notably Dali, Delvaux, Ernst, Lam, Tanguy and Magritte exhibit mythological incursions in their work. Surrealism sought to uncover new vistas of the imagination and it is reasonable to expect that if the Tree of Life framework with its mythological images were to have any claim whatever to representing a matrix of symbols of the Western psyche, these archetypes would manifest strongly in surrealist painting. The actual surrealist methods also bear strong comparison with those of Western magic.

Anna Balakian notes that in following the theories of Freud the surrealists found in automatic writing a form of 'self-administered psychoanalysis; placing themselves in a state of stupefying attentiveness, they tried to shut out all outside disturbances and to give free play to the inner powers of association of words and the images which these suggested . . . .'[1]

As we have already seen the contemporary magician similarly withdraws his attention from the external world to a meditative dimension where his language is one of ritual names of power and specific symbols, like Tarot arcana and Tattvas, for focusing the attention. The source-work 777 represents a body of associated mythological images arrived at by much the same process as that found in surrealism. One important difference however remains the concept of will. Automatic techniques require a total openness in the practitioner. The magicians of the Golden Dawn were given to structuring their inner journeys and employing protective techniques comparable to those found in yoga.

The surrealists, and their latter-day disciples, the supernatural realists, nevertheless share an aspiration which is also a hallmark of the current consciousness movement – a broadening of vision, an inquiry into the sources of inspiration and man's neglected powers of creativity, and a refusal to abide by the consensus logic of the day. The early Dadaists and Surrealists were revolutionaries in the true sense. Dadaist exhibitions were on occasion closed by police on the grounds that these new manifestations had nothing whatever to do with art.[2] Indeed, this period was host to a new vision which proposed to destroy the *status quo* by shattering it out of its complacency. The method of the new movement was undoubtedly anarchistic, but it was one of good-humoured insights – a challenge to the senses.

J. H. Matthews in his *Introduction to Surrealism* notes that 'the surrealist sees humour as the conjunction of the real and the fantastic; not only helping man resist the claims of the reality to which the world has accustomed him, but also placing within his reach the means to shake off habitual thought, thus permitting him to aspire to another form of reality, which answers another logic'.[3]

If the surrealists themselves found amusement in the way in which they demolished all faith in representational reality, the reaction of their audience was sometimes one of not taking the new art form too seriously. Hugh Philip, in a 1944 edition of *Angry Penguins*, wrote: 'surrealism is just a trick; quite a clever trick at times, but nonetheless a trick, which in this day of uncritical admiration, almost worship of the new, the original, the bizarre, has "caught on". . . .'[4]

From the standpoint of the 1970s it is now apparent that the surrealist mode which was, as Julien Levy put it, *a point of view*, has not been eclipsed by later fashions but has remained as one of the dominant styles in modern art. The graphic collages of Wilfried Satty and the supernatural realism of Viennese artists like Ernst Fuchs owe much to Max Ernst. Magritte's tamperings with physical perspective have found their way into numerous counter-culture graphics, among them the cover illustration for Carlos Castaneda's second volume *A Separate Reality*, and the works of Gervasio Gallardo, a contemporary fantasy illustrator. Modern advertising art shows that the visual effects evoked by the surrealists continue to prove effective as a means of arresting attention. Surrealism in fact achieves its result by appearing to represent an unfamiliar reality. Like contemporary forms of magic, surrealism takes us into locales where a new logic applies, where a new combination of images and symbols is presented in its own right. Matthews notes:[5]

The objects and creatures surrealism creates must impose themselves upon the imagination with all the conviction of truth – Ernst's hundred-headed woman, Breton's soluble fish and white-haired revolver or those strange encounters recorded so faithfully in the canvases of Delvaux, Magritte, Dali or Dorothea Tanning. The Surrealist invites his public to look before he asks them to understand. And he takes care to compel them to look, as dreams do, even when they have no expectation of understanding what they see. Thus the Surrealist – whether painter or poet – becomes in Eluard's phrase 'a slave to the faculty of seeing'.

The way of the modern shaman is to journey through the landscape of images knowing that they are as real as he wants them to be. He may become ensnared in hells expanded by his own fears and paranoia, or he may be entranced by heavenly visionary states of great beauty and splendour. The shaman can journey through symbolic locales which lead to his own transformation. The surrealist achievement was to indicate – for the first time with force since Bosch and Cranach – that reality extends to these domains, that the imagination encompasses all possibilities.

Several surrealists exhibit identifiable mythological content deriving from various archetypal energy sources, and accordingly express the surrealist world-view through different motifs and effects. It becomes possible to propose a three-fold division of the mythological images relating to the basic cosmology of earth, moon and sun.

For Magritte, the magic vision lies in rearranging an otherwise familiar reality so that flowers or pieces of fruit occupy a whole room or heavy objects float serenely in space, defying gravity. His orientation is Qabalistically associated with the physical world of Malkuth, and his technique hinges, like that of de Chirico, on perspective, shape and visual contrast.

Delvaux, Tanguy and Dali meanwhile emerge as predominantly lunar painters in the Qabalistic sense. Delvaux is the most obvious of these. Naked maidens walk through his pictures in trance-like reverie beneath the moon; his pictorial themes invariably revolve around the image of the White Goddess. Delvaux's nudes are milky-skinned, aloof, unblemished and often accompany death in the form of a skeleton. Sexual, serpentine trains pass near by but are never linked in any way to the frigid, silent women.

Tanguy meanwhile has made the symbol of the ocean one of personal significance. The moon is linked Qabalistically to the element water. Tanguy grew up in a mystical domain himself – the village of Locronan near the legendary Ys, which was said to have been engulfed in the fifth century when the daughter of King Gradlon formed an illicit love pact with the devil and opened the flood gates protecting the city from the sea. As a youth, Tanguy used to dive in the sea in search of bones and pebbles washed by the waves and there is a strong sense in his paintings of an ocean of hidden inner imagery. Tanguy's surreal land-scapes are often lunar grey and filled with an apparently reflected light such as that which has filtered through to the bottom of the ocean. His more elastic shapes have a suggestion of mutability to them, and in like fashion the lunar region of the unconscious, the Yesod of the Qabalists, suggests an ocean of forms and images constantly, like the tides, in a state of flux and transformation.

On the basis of the microcosm and macrocosm, the Tree of Life is also the Tree of Man (Adam Kadmon) and Yesod is superimposed upon the region of the genitals indicating that it also refers to the sexual impulses and fertility (another aspect of lunar worship, in witchcraft, for example).

While much of Salvador Dali's work is dream-like and elastic in quality (incorporating dripping clocks and pliable bodies), it is also extremely sexual. His *Young Virgin Auto-Sodomized By Her Own Chastity*, for example, involves a double play of images so that the young woman's limbs become aggressive penises. Marcel Jean has said of Dali's paintings that several are appropriate as 'illustrations of a kind for a still unwritten manual of psychoanalysis: even the titles sometimes provide a commentary with Freudian undertones. A predilection for suggestive or even remarkably unsymbolized sexual themes is notice-able in his work.'[6] Freud himself regarded Dali as the most significant of the surrealists, and their world-view hinges around the same primal sources in the unconscious.

While it is true that these surrealists – Tanguy, Delvaux, Magritte and Dali – to a large extent remained true to a dominant mythological energy source, the work of Max Ernst appears to embody marked transitions. His early work, such as that characterized by *The Elephant of the Celebes* (1921) is noticeably mechanistic, mirroring the Dadaist revolt against technology and its effects. Later paintings depict the savage forces inherent in nature and his work comes to represent a powerful, atavistic vision of man embroiled in nature's grasp. The last twenty years of Ernst's life, however, see a refinement of the harshness in his earlier work, and suggest a new-found calm. The mandala, a symbol of individuation or wholeness, features predominantly in his work, and suggests a centering absent for much of his artistic career. In Ernst's paintings, as with the medieval alchemists, we find a merging of opposites, of animal and human, of male and female. Even his mandala representations have two polarities; Paul Waldo-Schwartz in *Art and the Occult* makes the interesting observation that 'Ernst's suns are never wholly suns at all but equally lunar disks. They reflect rather than radiate, and end up as sigils of the great Zero wherein the solar—lunar, male—female union is mysteriously combined.'[7]

In the Tarot sequence we recall that the consciousness domain linking Yesod and Tiphareth, the lunar and solar centres, is represented by *Temperance*. This Tarot arcana represents a fusion of the elements, a gathering of resources and a harmonizing of influences, very much characteristic of Ernst's later work.

Malkuth is the Qabalistic entry into the unconscious mind and there is no doubt that of the transformers of physical reality towards a magical end, René Magritte is the supreme exponent. Magritte himself believed that painting was a magical act, and that the painter was endowed with superior powers. It has been said of him that 'Magritte behaves like God. He makes fire burn without consuming, puts boulders in the sky, pins clouds to the ground, turns men into stone, makes stone birds fly, forbids us to look upon his face . . . .'[8]

The motifs and representations in Magritte's paintings are familiar but his use of them is not. In *The Tomb of the Wrestlers* an evocative pink rose fills a room, and in *Personal Values* a huge comb and shaving brush rest on a miniature bed and wardrobe while leaning against the bedroom wall which is the sky. Magritte is able to shock us out of our everyday awareness by counterposing images: the face of a bowler-hatted man is obscured by an apple, while other such men are shown fashioned from clay and living in a world which is totally earthen. Elsewhere toes grow out of boots and breasts are superimposed upon a dress. Magritte is similarly a magician of context. In *The Childhood of Icarus* a jockey rides his horse through a large room in which there are framed pictures of the sky and the external face of a building. And true to defying gravity, Magritte depicts a huge boulder supporting a fortress floating carefree in the sky while waves below lap upon a beach (*The Castle of the Pyrenees*).

Magritte has said that magic is explicable only when it is utterly inexplicable, and his paintings bear this out. In *Ariadne's Thread*,

Magritte stressed that he also viewed his approach as akin to poetry:[9]

> assuming as real the poetic fact, if we try to discover its meaning we
> find a new orientation which immediately removes us from that
> barren region that the mind has ceased to fecundate. The object of
> poetry would become a knowledge of the secrets of the universe
> which would allow us to act on the elements. Magical transactions
> would become possible.

Among Magritte's magical images are a mermaid consisting of a
women's legs and the head and torso of a fish, a bird filled with sky,
and a man seated at a table – his head ablaze with white light.

The latter picture, *The Pleasure Principle*, recalls the magical technique
described in Carlos Castaneda's *Teachings of Don Juan*, of transferring
consciousness under willed imagination, to the head.[10] Like Carlos
Castaneda, Magritte was a city shaman. George Melly of the BBC
described him in 1965 as a secret agent, bent on bringing to disrepute
the whole apparatus of bourgeois reality. 'Like all saboteurs', said
Melly, 'he avoids detection by dressing and behaving like everybody
else.'[11]

While Magritte offers a magical interpretation of our familiar physical
world, and in this sense is very much a painter operating within
Malkuth consciousness, certain pictures embody a notion of implied
transcendence. *The Glass Key* is very much an earthen landscape –
depicting an isolated boulder positioned on the top of a heavy mountain
ridge. The picture is enthralling because it suggests that the boulder is
breaking with its origins – transcending its own state of density and
pointing aspiringly to the heavens.

Also, it should be noted that while Magritte deals in the language of
physical images, he does occasionally betray his mythological interests.
The Musings of a Solitary Walker shows a man strolling beside a river, but
in the foreground we are shown a figure deep in a somnabulistic
trance, strongly reminiscent of beliefs concerning the human double.
David Sylvester has referred to the intrusion of Egyptian influences on
L'Homme du Large which depicts dream images like hieroglyphic
inscriptions on a tomb, and in a fauvist painting, *The Image of the
Hermaphrodite* – itself a mystical symbol of union – we are shown the
bearded ocean god with a penis in the form of a woman.

In the work of Delvaux, Tanguy and Dali we find evidence of a
preoccupation with different aspects of the lunar consciousness of
Yesod, whether represented by astral, dream-like imagery, portrayals

of the White Goddess of lunar worship or strongly sexual allusions. Delvaux's women are usually entranced, as if sleep-walking. They are often naked, in procession, and convey a sense of magical ceremony. They walk beneath the moon, linked, it has been suggested, only by silence. For Marcel Jean, 'these women in lace gowns moving towards a triumphal vista of ancient buildings are all the same woman, duplicated, multiplied by invisible mirrors.'[12] We are never quite sure where we stand in Delvaux's pictures; his women especially seem aloof and withdrawn. We are not invited to participate in their ritual.

Delvaux insists on bringing his mythological women, however reminiscent of ancient Greece and Rome, into the twentieth century. *The Acropolis* and *The Cortege* both show processions of semi-clad maidens bearing lamps. Temples are visible, but other buildings are shown illuminated by gas lamp lighting. In *The End of the World* a group of young women stand on a pier overlooking a moonlit lake. Near by we notice a solitary railway carriage, suggesting that the mythological journey has come to an end.

Other works also show a fusion of traditional and contemporary world-views as if Delvaux is actively seeking to bring a magical aware-ness into the technological era. In *The Trolley, Red Door, Ephesus,* a tram courses its way along a street flanked by ancient temples, and whilst the trees which flourish in Delvaux's dream-time are in a natural setting, in *Christmas Night* trees grow near a railway yard in rows of pots. The woman perusing this scene is clothed, and in the context of Delvaux's other work, seems to be caught between the world of technological normality and a desire to act mythologically by shedding her clothing and regaining the status of a lunar wanderer.

In several of Delvaux's paintings Death takes a hand in the form of a skeleton. The latter is a bizarre metaphorical image of the 'inner man'. In Delvaux's view normal human beings are death stricken, while skeletons are expressive with their gestures. Persephone–Hecate and the Roman Diana are also associated with death, and Yesod is the first station in the underworld of the unconscious mind. It is not surprising that we find the death skeleton accompanying Delvaux's lunar worshippers in works like the famous *Sleeping Venus*. Delvaux deals in the polarities of life and death, classical and contemporaneous, sacred and profane, dream-like and physical. He invites us to expand our sense of causality by allowing both dimensions to occupy common ground, and proposes that the classical mythological sensibility be born again in each of us.

The paintings of Yves Tanguy, by contrast, are not overtly mytho-logical — they invariably depict smooth stylized objects and beings which have presence rather than personality — but they represent other facets of the lunar consciousness. Tanguy's symbols and motifs seem very much to suggest transition — objects becoming more real and requiring the creative mould of the ocean of formation upon them. His landscapes, in the lunar sense, are subject to the tides, and owe their very essence to the ocean, which as we have seen, is a basic cosmological image of spirit, space and causality. And while his early paintings like *The Mood of Now* and *With My Shadow* (both completed in 1928) have a definite organic feel to them and include limp fibrous growths and stem-like motifs, Tanguy's more mature works are markedly more abstract. James Thrall Soby has described his paintings in terms of the 'melting of land into the sky'[13] — Tanguy's flaccid forms seem to arise in an aspic dimension and often float in space, like newly conceived ideas.

Yesod is the energy source upon the Tree which pertains to this aspect of the creative process. Through it forms and images are channelled into the psyche en route to their final manifestation in Malkuth. The Tarot card *The Star*, which depicts the White Goddess with two flasks, transmitting the essence of a star into the waters of life upon the earth is similarly suggestive of the current and flow of creative ideas. In Tanguy's *A Large Picture which is a Landscape* (1917) we already have a clear preference for lunar greys, and the light in the picture is diffuse. In *The Lovers* his figures are rather like plasticine ghosts, with little shape or distinctiveness, and in the centre of the composition ambiguous shapes hover, free-form and unattached. The astral imagery of Tanguy's inner domain is characteristically shown in *The Rapidity of Sleep* where the planar objects join together almost like a sequence of memories from waking consciousness and taper off into a void of forgetfulness in the distance.

On the Tree of Life, the sephirah which flows into lunar Yesod is Hod, an energy vortex which supports the concepts of structure and form, and in particular stimulates rational design and mathematical formu-lation. Tanguy, while invariably elastic in his textures, nevertheless brings considerable structure into his later works, and in this sense appears to be interpreting the forces of Hod in a lunar context. *Indefinite Invisibility* (1942) sees a newly found mechanistic quality, reminiscent of science fiction machines which exhibit a positive structure but an elusive function, and the dolmen-like objects of *The Closing Days* are metallic in their sheen, rather like statues guarding the kingdom of an unknown intelligence. Tanguy elaborated his sense of intricate structures in works like *Rose of the Four Winds*, *The Transparent Ones* and *The Hunted Sky*, where his motifs are suggestive of hieroglyphics that etch themselves onto his object-shapes like a mysterious growth. *Multiplication of Arcs* was Tanguy's crowning work, and one which is unmistakably lunar. The landscape is populated by crowded rock formations, suggestive both of natural forms, and also a pervasive intelligence.

Tanguy, true to the lunar sense of transformation, never allows himself to be pinned down to a specific expression, with only one level of meaning. In his work we find a language of symbols which raises the paradox of their origin, and leaves us pondering the void from which they appear to precipitate. His later paintings, in quite a different way from that of Delvaux, nevertheless share that artist's sense of profound silence. Tanguy's horizon images gesture upwards into grey mysterious skies which taper off into another dimension and invariably his paintings seem lit with reflected light, enhancing fissures, textures and shadows. His is not the humanized expression of mythological archetypes but suggests instead their abstract qualities. Tanguy's later works are unquestionably 'hopeful'. His textured sentinels seem to await the dawning of a greater reality, and it is appropriate that his final painting *Multiplication of Arcs*, saw the most complete expression of his mysterious images made manifest.

Dali meanwhile, drawing on the traditions of Flemish art and psychoanalysis simultaneously, has rendered his images with more distinctiveness than Tanguy, and arguably with less mystery. Despite his dream images, Dali always has one foot in reality. He once proposed an experiment in which a colossal loaf of bread, fifteen yards long, would be baked and left early one morning in a public square in order to stimulate widespread incredulity. His so-called 'paranoia critical method' is based on visual puns, with the physical environment finding itself subject to hallucinatory interpretation. Like Magritte, Dali is a master of surprise, and has similarly taken it upon himself to fracture all sense of a bourgeois consensus reality. In a letter to Gala Eluard, later to be his wife, he wrote: 'I believe the moment is at hand when by a paranoiac and active advance of the mind, it will be possible (simultaneously with automation and other passive states) to systematize confusion and thus to help to discredit completely the world of reality.'[14]

Dali read Freud's *Interpretation of Dreams* and this revealed to him the whole dimension of repressed obsessions, neuroses and complexes which impinge on everyday behaviour. Dali was impressed by Freud's method of dream analysis as a means of expanding one's understanding of hidden aspects of the personality, and he became increasingly interested in insanity as an alternative world-view, much in the same fashion as R. D. Laing and Wilson Van Dusen.[15] In his painting *The Invisible Man* Dali builds his dream images meticulously, and they in turn form a suggested, or hidden image of the man himself, thereby 'giving pictorial expression to the way the insane impose double meanings on reality'.[16]

Like Magritte, Dali's shock effects invoke imagery from the physical world — the Qabalistic Malkuth — but his dream images are both elastic and hypersexual, characteristic of lunar Yesod. The sense of a fluid, astral dimension is very much apparent in works like *Hercules lifting the skin of the sea asks Venus for one moment longer before she awakens love* (1963). Hercules lifts the surface of the sea like a film and all the figures seem to be set, as if in a dream-like jelly. Dali's own *Soft Self Portrait* is a plasticine mask, propped up on crutches, and *The Great Masturbator* exhibits not only elasticity, but marked eroticism. A woman's head and a man's genitals emerge from an amorphous plastic/organic sculpture; it is very much a case of the dream made tangible. In so many of Dali's works one can feel the texture, catch hold of the culprit image which is the key to parallel dimensions.

Paintings like *The Temptation of Saint Anthony*, with its bizarre insect/elephant processions, and *One second before awakening from a dream caused by the flight of a bee around a pomegranate*, characterize Dali's living nightmare. Yesod is the astral realm of dreams and memories which pertain to the individual ego. We have only begun to impinge on a more universal archetypal consciousness in these pictures. On Dali's own admission, his work relates primarily to the subconscious of the individual and, true to Freud's direction, dwells more with individual repressions and neuroses rather than any transcendental Jungian notion of a Collective Unconscious.

Dali's religious phase produced his most shamanistic painting. In *Santiago El Grande* the Christian hero mounted on the cosmic horse rises towards the vaults of the crystal heavens. Christ appears transfixed in space and radiating light, some distance above him. This particular excursion into supernatural realism very much epitomizes the new direction which has since emerged in the mid-1970s — the search for a powerful spiritual mythology and its artistic depiction in realistic and non-abstract images.

There have always been magical elements in surrealism as a result of the visionary journey into the unconscious, and the artist's meandering in the forest of symbols. We think of Victor Brauners's paintings teeming with occult familiars, Felix Labisse's animal/human trans- formations and Wolfgang Paalen's totemic landscapes. Wilfredo Lam, in particular, has embodied in his work the concept of the unconscious as an infinite source of awe and wonderment which can inspire the artist to great heights. He had seen the fantastic images of Bosch and Bruegel in the Prado after leaving his native Cuba for the first time in 1923. In 1940 he joined the Surrealist Movement, and after its dispersion (Dali, Tanguy and Ernst to the United States, Paalen to Mexico) Lam returned to Cuba. He visited Haiti four years later and was initiated into the voodoo ecstasy cult of Vevers. The voodoo practitioner seeks to elevate his spirit to the level of the *loa* divinities, to embody their uplifting energies through the act of physical possession. Lam demonstrates in his work the common ground occupied by visionary art and magic. He has been a wanderer among the spirit beings who dwell deep in the jungle of the human unconscious, a shaman worshipper among both devils and divinities, gods themselves half human, half vegetable, and very much images of transformation. Lam has said of the forest that it represents 'that world without limits with the mystery of its space indefinitely prolonged beyond the veil of its tree-trunks and leaves'.[17]

Lam's personal cultural heritage is enormously multi-faceted. His mother was a mix of African, Indian and European, his father Cantonese. From his contact with surrealists onwards he came to stress the nature of his art as an expression of the inner journey, and allied his pictorial techniques with that of automatism – direct and unimpeded contact with the unconscious. 'In my canvases', he once said, 'I transmit all that is essential in the interior of my being.'[18]

This being so, we discover a vast range of images and forces lurking in the psyche of the Cuban surrealist. Horned, bird-head humans with fierce teeth, claws and daggers, warrior steeds, creatures with ritual gestures who blend back into the forest having appeared for an instant, totemic insignia – all of these throng his paintings, and have made works like *The Jungle* and *The Eternal Present* justly famous. Lam's paintings have extraordinary force, and his graphic interest in ritual sigils, especially those found in Voodoo ceremonial, flow into his compositions so that they become an invocation in their own right. Lam's painting of the Voodoo god of thunder Oggum Ferraille (or Ogoun Feraille) draws on personal visions derived from Voodoo techniques of ecstasy. His conviction that at 'a level of the mind deeper than the reasoning faculty desire awakens'[19] is reminiscent of the surreal English trance artist Austin Spare, one-time disciple of the occultist Aleister Crowley. Spare, like the Voodoo practitioners, entered trance states in which he would deliberately seek union with the hidden atavistic images of his mind – in his case images he believed to be animal memories of a previous incarnation.[20] Lam, like Spare, constantly portrays the human transforming into the animalian, or fusing with the branches and foliage of the jungle. His art is alive with totemic images illuminated, like Tanguy's paintings, by a diffuse ethereal light.

Like Lam, Max Ernst – among the most cosmic of the surrealists – has had recourse to the symbol of the forest. However, while much of Lam's preoccupation is with visually invoking the spirit forces which lurk therein, a recurrent theme in Ernst's work has been transcendence. His sympathy is with the bird, another highly personal symbol, who rises above the melange of nature spirits and demons and takes refuge in the sun.[21]

Ernst, like Tanguy and Lam, grew up in a magical, evocative environment. He was intrigued by the vastness of the Black Forest, which seemed to him to represent an infinite dimension and a great source of hidden mystery. The noted medieval occultist Cornelius Agrippa wrote his famous treatises in Cologne, only six miles from Ernst's birthplace, Bruhl, and when he was nearly fifteen an event occurred which for Ernst was truly magical. His pet pink cockatoo died suddenly, and almost immediately a sister was born into his family. As a result of this synchronistic occurrence, Ernst became deeply interested in occult matters; it seemed to him that he had witnessed a type of transformation.

Ernst's early compositions are highly mechanistic. *Winter Landscape: The Asphyxiation* (1921) shows pipes and furnaces beneath the level of the ground throwing pollution into the air and causing the branches of a tree to wither. His famous *Elephant of the Celebes* is a mockery of ugliness – his monster being a grotesque, furnace-like creature devoid of any aesthetic function. Its neck lunges forward like a dangling pipe, its tusks are misplaced and its legs resemble truncated stumps. The creature responds to a gesture from a headless human being.

Ernst soon heeded the call of the forest and its bird life as basic visual images of his response to the environment. True to his Dadaist reaction against technology, his *Little tear gland that says tic tac* does include a representation of the forest but his sun is a tooth-edged metallic gear wheel. As a reminder that many of the forces of Ernst's psyche were still trapped from full expression, his *Dove* (1928) is depicted behind the bars of a cage.

Max Ernst soon embarked on a number of pictures which showed both the dynamism and destructiveness inherent in nature. In *The Joy of Living* we are shown luxuriant vegetation, but on closer examination discover anthropomorphic creatures lurking there, one with pointed human fingers and sharp needle teeth. Several works show a solar or lunar disc transcendent over a putrefied earth, *Grey Forest*, and a number of paintings entitled *The Entire City* in particular. A gradual direction emerges in his artistic career towards identification with the disc or mandala itself, a symbol of the reconciliation of opposing forces both within the mind and the external environment.

Ernst had a visionary approach to creativity from an early time in his life. He notes in *Beyond Painting* that since the age of five he had been able to exercise a remarkable capacity for seeing more than would normally be apparent to the casual observer. A wooden panel painted with black strokes on a ruddy field to imitate mahogany provoked what Ernst has called 'associations of organic forms (a threatening eye, long nose, huge bird's head with thick black hair)'. [22] In August 1925, while resting in an inn at Pornic near the sea coast, Ernst gazed down at the accentuated grain of the wooden floor boards and excitedly began to take tracings of the grain with a soft pencil. 'I was surprised', he writes, 'at the sudden intensification of my visionary faculties and at the hallucinatory succession of contradictory images being super-imposed on each other with the persistence and rapidity of amorous memories.' Later he explored other materials and textures – leaves, cloth, thread – 'my eyes perceived human heads, various animals, a battle ending in a kiss [*Bride of the Wind*], rocks [*The Sea and the Rain, Earthquake, The Sphinx in her Stable*].' [23]

The textural surfaces on which Ernst fixed his gaze became for him a leaping-off point, a catalyst to his imaginative endeavours. In this sense they resembled the sigils upon which Austin Spare meditated while entering a state of trance, for they too were catalysts to an amazing outpouring of energy from the unconscious. [24]

Ernst named his process frottage, and he found that gradually the specific textures became subordinate to the images which manifested through the process. He had discovered a way of rendering invisible potencies tangible in the light of day. Like Spare, Ernst referred to forces operating through him – 'the method excludes conscious mental guidance . . . reducing to a minimum the active part of what has hitherto been called the "author" of the work . . . .'[25]

For Ernst, the artist was not an originator so much as one who is present at the birth of his work. And like the magician, with profound respect for the forces and images inherent in the vast archives of the mind, Ernst saw his role as requiring direct entry into the symbolic inner domains which would inspire him:[26]

> every normal person (and not only the 'artist') carries in his
> subconscious an inexhaustive supply of buried pictures and it is a
> matter of courage or of liberating methods (such as automatic writing)
> to bring to light from expeditions into the unconscious unforged
> (uncoloured by control) objects (pictures) . . . .

Ernst's philosophy quite clearly embraces the shaman's world-view. The surrealist journey is into inner spaces and dimensions which will yield powerful and expressive images of a greater reality. Like the shaman's direct sojourn with the gods of his culture in a quest for meaning, Ernst was similarly engaged in finding 'the myth of his time'.[27]

The Robing of the Bride (1939) remains one of his most impressively occult paintings and depicts semi-human creatures who seem intent on a macabre esoteric ceremony. The central figure – the bride herself – wears an owl's mask, suggestive of transformation into animal forms, and her richly textured robe is highly ritualistic. A bird-headed man near by holds a menacing sword and a curious four-breasted amphibious creature (the anticipated fruit of their union?) nestles pathetically on the floor.

Ernst invoked strange gods in *The Antipope*, again a representation of human and animal atavisms, and very much characteristic of the style adopted by the later fantasy artists of the Vienna school, notably Ernst Fuchs.

In later years the paintings of Max Ernst acquired a more cosmic nature and his images had a strong direction towards transcendence, which had not been present during the more tormented phases of his life.

The Marriage of Heaven and Earth, completed in 1962, finds the sky encapsulated by the folds of the yellow earth in a beautiful mandala design of great force and simplicity, and in his homage to the obscure astronomer E. Wilhelm Tempel, Ernst produced some of his most breathtaking creations. The revised edition of *Maximiliana* (1975), which saw the collaboration of Ernst with Peter Schamoni, was indicative of the continuing preoccupation Ernst had at this time with cosmic symbols of the earth, the sea, the sky and planetary constellations. An exquisite luminescent mandala was accompanied by the following poem:

> *The Sun*
> I am no black circle
> I am no white square
> I am no blue haze
> I am heaven
> I am hell
> I am the bridal bed of heaven and hell
> I am the spouse of all planets
> The elements radiate the resplendence of my love.

This painting and others like it are especially suggestive of the Tiphareth sphere of consciousness which represents the regenerative, solar aspects of consciousness, the mandala of light in spiritual man. Tiphareth is the domain of the sun gods – Apollo, Osiris, Christ – in the classical cosmologies – and provides in man an inner centering similar to the sun's position in the galaxy as the focal point of planetary rotations. In the Qabalah it is an energy source of love, new life and harmony, characteristics invariably ascribed to the great solar deities of mythology.

Ernst's vision, in a sense, transcended that of the other surrealists because while much of the effect in surreal imagery was to shock and disturb the observer – thus shaking him out of his limiting concepts of everyday reality – Ernst perhaps more than any of his peers, offered a solution of inner reconciliation.

The mythological journey of the shaman is one which takes us through the imagery of earth, and lessons comparable to those of Castaneda's Don Juan – the venture between the cracks in the worlds – are revealed by the visual jugglery of 'physical' surrealists like Magritte. Dali, Tanguy and Delvaux in different ways, have gravitated to the lunar domain of consciousness, the world of reflections, dreams and hallucinations. Ernst remains a solitary exponent among those of the

Surrealist and Dadaist persuasions, of the transcendental solar function.

We are host at the present time to a dramatic revival of the issues which underlay the whole Surrealist Movement. Just as Breton and his followers sought an extension of the limits of reality – a fully fledged incursion into the psyche – so too, as I have already indicated, we find at present an increasing preoccupation with the nature of human potential creativity and expanded forms of consciousness. Stanley Krippner has suggested that the development of interest in the healthy individual rather than the neurotic, which occurred with the birth of humanistic psychology, has had much to do with this new direction. Transpersonal psychology, with its stress on states of mind which transcend ego-oriented levels of awareness has certainly grown out of earlier forms of growth therapy and gestalt psychology and in particular the work of Carl Rogers, Abraham Maslow and Fritz Perls.[28]

While transpersonal psychologists like Charles Tart, Montague Ullman, John Lilly and Stanislav Grof have begun to investigate mythological states of mind within the realm of consciousness research, it is abundantly clear that the surrealists were early pioneers on this inner journey.

We live in a highly communicative era, ornamented and assailed by audio-visual media like placards, poster art and product advertising. As I hope to show, record cover albums, posters and current trends in modern painting reflect in some measure the surrealist approach to the external world.

Like the magicians of the Golden Dawn in their pursuit of tangible inner spaces, our current fantasy realists are proposing new mythological locales on the borderland of human consciousness. Once again we are asking for our world-view to be jolted out of its technological constrictions.

In writing of voodoo, Joseph Campbell mentioned a Haitian expression: 'When the anthropologist arrives, the gods depart.'[29] The same of course may be said of modern technology which has, in theory, banished any need for gods and mysteries and has placed in their stead equations, formulae and the fruits of mechanical enterprise.

Certain elements of our youth culture, the fantasy artists included, seem to be calling for the gods to return.

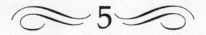

Magic and fantasy – the new visionary art

Psychedelic art flowered in the by-ways and enclaves of Haight Ashbury, a visual manifestation of the mind-altering drug-consumer culture which emerged in the mid-1960s. Like the forms of enhanced sensory consciousness which it reflected, early psychedelic art, particularly that which embellished rock concert posters, was vivid and organic, owing much to the art nouveau of Beardsley and the earlier Viennese style of Mucha. Words and images merged into each other, against a field of dazzling colours and optical effects.

One of the best psychedelicists, Peter Max, certainly reflected the counter-cultural mystical interests of this period – in works like his *Prana Buddha* poster printed on an offset grid of green fading into orange and claret red, and his dramatic *Zodiac* series for NBC television.[1] Max's graphic style, like that of Milton Glaser and Heinz Edelmann – producer of the remarkable visuals in the Beatle film *Yellow Submarine* – depended mostly on planes of contrasting colour. Its impact resulted more from bombarding the senses with hallucinatory images than from captivating and enticing the viewer.

By comparison the current direction towards supernatural realism seems to extend the boundaries opened during the psychedelic period. The art of the on-going consciousness actually posits an alternative reality, a symbolic domain in which the observer is invited to participate. The new fantasy art is three – and perhaps even four – dimensional, while its psychedelic predecessor was predominantly two-dimensional. Like the surrealists, the exponents of the emergent style are extending the physical dimension towards the mythic and archetypal domains rather than exploding the energy of the unconscious in a barrage of graphic forms, as tended to be the case in the 1960s. And while the psychedelic years saw an exploring of new levels of mind, and with it a new-found interest in Eastern and Western mysticism, the current mood seems to me to be both more reflective and more informed. There are signs at present of a new mythology in fantasy art, a proposed mystical basis for a more permanent and enduring visionary reality.

Some of the art of the transitionary period appeared in José and Miriam Argüelles's fine book *Mandala*. The Argüelles themselves had spent several years examining graphically the optical potential and effects of mandala images and the result was a multi-coloured geometricism which hovered somewhere between 1960s psychedelics and Vasarely's optical geometry, while also suggesting markedly the colours and energies associated with chakras and mystical fields of force. 'Mandala of the Octave' which grows outward from a central pulsing source and the extraordinary 'The Mage must move across the earth' are mirrored in style by the more recent graphic works of Abdul Mati Klarwein which place chakra and Kundalini-type energy currents against a backdrop of three-dimensional realism. While 'Circulation of the Light' is beautifully intricate, including in its patterns delicate purple, buff and orange textures and kaleidoscopic geometry, it presents a pattern rather than an alternative locale.

Other work of 'cosmic geometry' included in the volume – Matiello's 'Golden Egg' and 'Game of Spheres' – present a similar sense of distance. However Dion Wright's superb 'Mandala of Evolution', which depicts an ocean of primeval marine and plant forms merging into an ancient jungle of forgotten bird and animal species, provides an example of the new direction towards supernatural realism.

The work of Spanish artist Gervasio Gallardo, for example (especially paintings like *A Fine and Private Place* with its bowler-hatted figure and dice players, fashioned out of stone), owes an obvious debt to Magritte and perhaps also Labisse. But paintings like *The Wedding* which depicts a mallard-headed bridegroom, and *Aliens 4* with its child head composed of flower blooms, retain an element of naivety and sentimentality which mark him aside from mainstream supernatural realism.

The same is also true of Patrick Woodroffe's *Mythopoeikon*, a collection of surreal and psychedelic works spanning ten years which were used to illustrate book and record sleeves, posters and children's stories.

Woodroffe, a colleague of Roger Dean's, clearly sees himself as a mythmaker – as a collector of images pertinent to what he sees around him as the nightmare of an all-encompassing technology. For him, the solution is the creation of an alternative visual mythology – a return to fantasy forms and science fiction and the memories of childhood. Woodroffe writes: 'There are two worlds for every man. He has his day to day world of quiet routine in unpredictable nature – a leisurely tightrope walk over a cataract of tragedy.' In a manner reminiscent of Carlos Castaneda's Don Juan – haunted by death lurking over his left shoulder – Woodroffe continues:[2]

> The rope's end – death – hangs in the air like a short branch. And any step of the way he may slip, fall and perish in real agonies; real beasts wait to devour him.
>
> But as he walks he may close his eyes and retreat into a world enclosed within the walls of his skull, a world confined to tiny electric pathways between billions of minute brain cells.
>
> Fantastic art is the cartography of this nowhere-land. And we may see familiar places there – familiar faces too. We all know this nowhere – the joy we feel is the joy of recognition, of rediscovery.

Woodroffe is clearly a visual mythmaker – a rediscoverer of forgotten or neglected images. He acknowledges his debt to the work of Salvador Dali, Bosch and the Viennese school of fantastic realism, and his images suggest that he sees his purpose as a depicter of a modern shamanism:[3]

> Ideas slowly began to flow. The music of Gustav Mahler and Anton Bruckner – those ecstatic and inexorable symphonies – flashed new images in my mind. The instruments of the orchestra spoke with the voices of birds, fish and fabulous beasts.

Woodroffe's world is populated by fish-legged women, ferocious serpents, tentacled devils and horned satyrs. His images seem to bubble just below consciousness, ready to burst out into the everyday world. Woodroffe's mythology seems at the present, however, to be a predominantly aggressive and destructive one. Unlike Roger Dean, there is no sense of emergence or inward security in his work and in many ways it still reflects the bombastic psychedelic style of the 1960s. Unlike Gallardo, Woodroffe's sentimentality is somewhat cynical – his women are often like dolls – plastic, manufactured products – and his mythical beasts and fantasy guardians are armed with machine-guns or other savage weapons.

Like Woodroffe, American-based Abdul Mati Klarwein is best known through the commercial application of his work. His intricate, multi-coloured, high-energy paintings have adorned the record sleeves of several albums by jazz trumpeter Miles Davis and rock group Santana. But he is also linked to other traditions. Much of his finest work is housed in the Aleph Sanctuary in the Ernst Fuchs Museum, Vienna, – Fuchs himself being a notable visionary in the fantastic art movement.

Klarwein's cosmology is a mixed one: idyllic, aristocratic negroes, meditating swamis, bikinied sunbathers and triple-headed goddesses stride side by side, while in the distant horizon perhaps an Islamic temple or tribal totem rises into the sky. The cover illustration of his first volume, *Milk N' Honey*, depicts an aleph atop a mystical light-shrouded mountain, and segments of the Qabalistic Tree of Life. Included in the book is a superb example of pantheistic realism — a Judaic mandala superimposed dramatically over a verdant garden-wilderness. Klarwein advocates a tantric alchemical view of the world which involves a rediscovery of one's total being. A clear macrocosm–microcosm fusion is implied in his proposal that 'when perception is directed towards the body one can clear the nerves, and the pulse of the rhythm of the universe has the same pulse as the person'.[4] Klarwein's murals are frequently hyper-erotic. His vision of unity and totality is almost an all-encompassing expression of the sexual drive — of forms interpenetrating and fusing; of life as a transcendental fertility rite.

One of his paintings shows a lunar silver-haired woman aflame with a Kundalini fire-bodied man pulsing inside her — a modern depiction of the King–Queen heavenly androgyne concept in medieval alchemy. Meanwhile Klarwein's free-form commentary suggests a kaleidoscopic flurry of energy forces, weaving and transforming in the universal cosmic dance:[5]

> the dervish Hora creates such a whirlwind of magnetic energy that
> even other conscious creatures like spirit-world demiurges,
> Olympian gremlins and Hindu deities appear en masse amongst
> and inside the ever-growing, concentric circles of the free sweating
> dancers, while thousands of children, shrieking with joyous
> laughter find themselves gliding through the air like exalted
> swallows before the rain.

If Klarwein is a tantric he is also a surrealist, a lover of paradox and jest. The commentary to his recent volume *God Jokes* is minimal, but like the Zen Koans, succinct:

> I'm going to turn into a dream,
> And then you'll be in real trouble.

— and humorously perceptive

> There used to be a great tension between my rational and
> irrational selves. However a few years of rationalizing,

92

My rational self has rationalized itself
Right into the irrational,
And now I'm finally in harmony with myself . . . .

And there is no question that he regards himself as a modern shaman:
'Ecstasy', he writes, 'is my frame of reference.'

Klarwein represents a strong tendency to portray visually an
alternative sensory reality and it is this which has led Robert Masters
and Jean Houston to identify him with the branch of fantastic realism
which owes most to surrealism – rather than with the purely graphic
forms of psychedelic art. It seems that what emerges in the new school
is an increasing tendency to depict symbolic and mythical landscapes
as if they were ongoing realities. This three-dimensional realism, as I
have already suggested, was markedly understressed in the earlier
forms of psychedelic art, while the new effect is one of allurement – of
entering a fantastic and mythological realm which gives meaning and
awe to the everyday social reality, and transforms it.

In California during recent years, a publishing company named
Pomegranate has been instrumental in issuing reproductions of some
of the most remarkable visionary paintings yet to appear in this genre.
As with Gallardo, surrealism and the art of the psychedelic 1960s
continues to exercise a prime influence but the sense of transcendence
and renewal – the visionary aim of Eden regained – is also implied.
The artists themselves are little-known technicians of a meticulous
style of painting, among the most proficient being artists like Gage
Taylor, Bill Martin and Cliff McReynolds.

Walter Hopps, Curator at the Smithsonian Institution, has described
the movement as an integrative offshoot of the earlier spontaneous,
counter-culture period:[6]

I was seeing the germinal work of young, profoundly serious, and as
yet unknown artists. From the splintering light and explosive
possibilities of the counter-culture that flourished in San Francisco
during the late 60's, they were emerging with their spirits and
energies intact, now at a moment when that culture appeared to
have already peaked and passed its high point. As the dream of
those years seemed to be fading from those of us who had believed
in it and watched it with admiration, some came forth who had been
a part of it, and lived it, assimilating its philosophies and its forms,
coalescing that experience into a concrete vision.

The styles within this grouping are representational, stylistic and in some instances photo-realistic. One artist, Thomas Akawie, has chosen to concentrate almost totally on imagery derived from Egyptian mythology.

An overriding consideration however is unity with the environment, an integrated cosmology of man within the universe, a regaining of the sacred on earth. Cliff McReynolds's *A New Earth (11 Peter 3:13)* is clearly apocalyptic; it depicts a crystal river coursing through a paradise garden in which human beings, animals and birds are equally at home. In the distance an ethereal cosmic tree rises majestically into the sky as a type of sacred totem.

Bill Martin's *Autumn*, in a manner similar to that of Maxfield Parrish, is similarly idyllic — bronzed and autumnal trees, elegant white herons, a naked child playing in the stream — subject matter far removed from the metropolis. Meanwhile Martin's *Rock* depicts a domed stone which rises up out of a welcoming grassy field. A natural fountain of pure water comes out of the top of the dome, producing four rivulets in a sacred, cross-like configuration. Martin's work suggests a mythological dimension rendered visibly, a merging of the symbolic and the real. McReynolds's *Landscape With Hand Grenade* depicts metaphorically the choice of modern mechanistic and urban man. He may either pursue values inherently destructive or seek to regain a more integrative consciousness — a unity of man with nature and her manifestations. Within visible distance of the domineering grenade, figures dance in a grassy field adulating a flower. A procession of parents and children emerge from the ground almost as if at the end of a journey of transformation. Martin's *Garden of Life* and Taylor's *Mescaline Woods* similarly propose the option for harmonized, natural existence.

It is easy to dismiss these art works as clichéd forms of nostalgia, but it is rather less obvious that they endeavour to identify a mythological basis for Western society. Theodore Roszak's contention that modern man is currently in search of the 'visionary sources of his being' very aptly fits the mood of this emergent art style. And, as with Klarwein, the paradox is to express the principle of the microcosm and the macrocosm both inwardly and outwardly.

British graphic artist Roger Dean poses the same paradox but in a different manner. His art work for record album covers sees a constant flux between the organic forms of nature and the mechanistic constructs of the automated world. Dean's own solution is an extension of his interest in fantasy illustration: the environment and especially the buildings one dwells in should be constructed to reflect a sense of the elemental forces in nature. Dean's preoccupation is with a more total reality. Close colleague Donald Lehmkuhl writes of Dean:[7]

> He shows us insects with nuclear power, fish swimming in air, waterfalls without a source. He fuses Stonehenge with spacecraft and gives elephants wings. He goes out of this world, out of perceived reality. He pursues the incomparable. Where he goes is also reality. His work is about this reality: about the nature of things, of forms, of appearances, of feelings, spiritual feelings. Feelings which (like music) are themselves both perceptions and stirred memories of places, events, creations long ago, or — more likely — long ahead . . . . Dean's work is about the mind in matter, about the unaccountability of form, about the visibility, invisibility of energy, about the inscrutability of space.

In Dean's more aggressive illustrations his flying machines are like menacing birds of prey which threaten to lay waste the world beneath them and his winged elephants soar through crimson skies like bomber aircraft. Meanwhile, non-human, armour-plated warriors stride vengefully through his landscapes producing an effect of chaos and alarm.

By contrast Dean's idyllic pictures show organic habitats rising out of the earth, in harmony with its textural forms. His glaciers suggest beautiful sculptures, reindeers dwell on grassy verges enveloped in an ethereal mist while medieval knights make their way into a fortress which shimmers like crystal. Fish swim through space with unusual expressions in their eyes, as if dominated by a magnetic force given off by the sacred pyramid structure in the distance.

Dean's world is paradoxical but it respects nature's energies, and his archetypal heroes are magicians or creators of fantastic organic machines which harness the universal life-force constructively. Like the California school, Dean's fantasy art is such that he graphically depicts alternative modes of being, which in themselves have evolved out of a more mature and less exploitative view of the world. Dean's magic is a natural attunement to the pulse of life and form. His approach, however, is very much to relate these understandings to practicalities — to man as a functioning being in a social environment. Consequently he expresses his world-view through images like aircraft, buildings, transport vehicles and other manifestations of technology, while implying that man's creations would do well to be in harmony with the broader source of meaning and reality apparent in the world.

While much of the art of the fantasy revival reflects an integrative response, a vision as it were of man in a more organic and illuminating environment, some artists operating within the genre have presented a particularly hostile alternative reality in their work. H. R. Giger's art has a demonic immediacy about it – eerie, ashen textures, vaults of bones and machinery and supernatural entities are shown shrouded in a hazy light. Limbs are depicted riveted to metallic crosses in a savage mockery of ritual death. Snakes weave in and out of zomboid skulls, and the artist's women are particularly prey to an evil presence which seems to trap them in a mesh of hostile images. Works like Giger's *The Spell* represent a very real and terrifying inner space in which the bone-like vault has the effect of enclosing the consciousness of the observer. Giger's vision is especially convincing because in Lilly's sense he demonstrates the immediacy of the symbolic terrain of the paranoid imagination. There is no escaping from Giger's world – no sense of transcending the 'limits' of the inner landscape in which the occult prison walls are so graphically real. Giger shows us a world with terrifying forces impinging inwards upon its victims – of human beings overcome by a trance-like reverie, trapped in a hell-state where machinery and organic forms weld themselves into an enclosing, aggressive net of images. In the Qabalistic sense his work is Qlippothic – the obverse aspect of the integrative energies of the Tree of Life. And yet Giger's is an authentic, almost transcendental evil. Evil in the sense of a powerful emotional energy state – a constricting and terrifying polarity of the creative imagination.

Ernst Fuchs, however, presents a curious blend of positive and negative imagery in a surreal style which owes as much to modern occult philosophy as it does to the classical styles of the Renaissance. An important figure in the contemporary Austrian fantasy school (which also includes painters like Rudolf Hausner, Karl Korab and Erich Brauer), Fuchs was born in Vienna in 1930. After 1945 he spent several years studying at the Academy of Fine Arts in Vienna, and later founded his own gallery to encourage young artists operating within the same fantasy genre. Although much of Mati Klarwein's work is housed in the Galerie Alexander Braumuller in Paris, several of Klarwein's most important murals are displayed in the Aleph Sanctuary of Fuch's museum in Vienna. Fuch's own work is often apocalyptic. In his *Satan's Heaven* triptych of 1954, the central panel features a host of grotesque trumpeters heralding the ominous presence of death itself.

A bevy of alien misshapen heads flanked by skulls and bones presents itself as a terrifying witness of the last hours. Meanwhile on the left-hand side a sword-bearing warrior stands atop a disembodied head, and on the right a winged multi-limbed insect seems to be encroaching snare-like, upon a radiating mandala form, as if about to snatch its last light for food.

Fuch's beatific paintings, like his *Child Playing With an Angel in the Desert* and *Crucifixion* both present more orthodox religious symbolism, but his figures nevertheless seem to glisten with a magnetic presence that is more magical than religious. *Joyous Rosary* (1958-61) presents Christ almost as a glyph – like the symmetrical Adam Kadmon astride the holy pentagram – and his wings and cloak are jewelled and ornamented in such a way that Christ is more a texture, more a pantheistic fabric of the heavens, than a tangible being. In a more recent work, *Transformed Gods*, one of Fuch's figures is a skull-headed wizard, crowned with the Pope's regalia. In his left hand he holds a ritual object – an egg within an egg – and in his right a golden wand, which, like a sabre, pierces and kills a dragon at his feet. Fuch's super-natural personae have magical power – they are beings who control the imagery of their domain in the same way that the occultist endeavours to discipline the symbolic imagery of his shamanistic journey. Meanwhile his *Unicorn's Wedding* explores the concept of occult polarities. An anthropomorphic creature with a unicorn's head takes the hand of a naked maiden whose golden hair is embellished with white ostrich feathers. While several hideous, imputed offspring grovel beneath them, a luminous astral form also begins to take shape between the unicorn–atavism and his bride. Fuchs appears to offer in his paintings a magical alternative. We have within us a pantheon of magical and religious images which at different times reveal strange and contrasting facets of an inner symbolic reality. We can pursue the force or current which is the essence of the magical imagination, or we can continue to revere the outer shell of these realities – shown to us in the power-based institutions of orthodox religion. Fuchs is forever painting figures that seem to be shells and, like Giger, uses the skull as a symbol of a veneer which houses a much more potent inner reality.

Four artists more than any others, capture the facets of the new magical consciousness: Diana Vandenberg, Johfra Bosschart, Wilfried Satty and Rosaleen Norton.

Diana Vandenberg and Johfra Bosschart combine a sort of psychedelic realism with magical imagery and much of their work has appeared as large-format posters. Their art contains recurrent Hermetic and Rosicrucian symbolism and belongs to the European school of fantastic realism which owes much to the surrealism of artists like Dali, Magritte, and Labisse in particular.

Wilfried Satty's collages, now well known particularly on the West coast of the United States, also link the contemporary consciousness with earlier surrealist forms. Satty is very much of the 1970s, but his collage technique is reminiscent of Max Ernst and his Dadaist contemporaries, who were similarly preoccupied with presenting graphically an alternative reality that challenged man's sense of certainty within his own domain, and stretched the imagination to its limits.

Rosaleen Norton, a former colleague of Australian artist Norman Lindsay, is both artist and practising witch. Her art depicts an impressive cosmology based on her own ritual and meditative practices. Animal–human deities and vortexes of energy throng her pictures, many of which antedate by several years the new supernatural realism.

Diana Vandenberg and Johfra Bosschart

Diana Vandenberg was born in The Hague in 1923, and christened Angèle Thérèse Blomjous. Between 1941 and 1943 she studied in the Academy of Fine Arts, coming into contact with a number of artists who had been influenced by Eastern mystical ideas. She also trained under Francine van Davelaar, who was herself an anthroposophist. In 1946 she met Franciscus Johannes Gijsbertus van den Berg – later to be her husband. Thankfully he has chosen to shorten his lengthy name taking Johfra Bosschart as his artistic nom de plume! His style of painting is in many ways like hers – stylized and evocative but owing much of its impact to a sense of the theatrical. Like Labisse, his early landscapes had an organic geometry to them. His figures were often wide-eyed and alluring but only partially convincing. His later work, such as his Zodiac paintings and his excellent triptych *Unio Mystica* has captured a much more impressive cosmic presence.

He and Angèle, or Diana as she now called herself, formed a friendship with a Mr C. L. J. Damme who introduced them to an offshoot of Max Heindel's American Rosicrucian group. Diana found its cosmology exciting. She also studied the Hermetic philosophy of the legendary Smargardine Tablet and its teachings concerning the microcosm and macrocosm.

The concepts of Hermeticism were transposed into her paintings.

98

Rex et Regina and *Rex et Regina II* both depict the alchemical marriage, pertaining here of course to Diana and Johfra themselves. Their heads are shown against verdant surroundings symbolic of nature and growth. Diana's head appears more Egyptian, with well-defined cheek bones and a regal brow. Johfra acquires the characteristics of a Greek sage with a long, curling beard.

While the heads, like statues, dominate the terrain, their gaze is inward, their expressions meditative. But characteristically a close examination of the heads shows that they are joined together in the same way that the medieval alchemists depicted the King and Queen joined into one body as a symbol of transcendental unity.

If there is a fault in Diana Vandenberg's work it is a tendency towards an almost self-conscious inclusion of mystical symbols in her work. In her early paintings her motifs – hovering spheres, luminescent crystals and stylized temples flanked by mythological animals – seemed to be rearranged more like a grammar of images rather than as an esoteric script revealing its mysteries.

One work of this type shows the conflict of a triple-winged fire-bird representative of the divinity in man, combating a similarly triple-winged dragon symbolizing thought experience and sexual desire – a painting necessarily labouring the cosmological three-fold division of man. Her more recent Graal imagery however is more potent, over-flowing with rich golden light.

Diana Vandenberg's paintings appear at first glance to belong to the late psychedelic period – their colours are rich and abundant, her use of textures and form, carefully delineated with considerable attention to detail. In 1968 Diana wrote a letter to the famous occult magazine *Planete* in response to an article which had appeared on the mystical connotations of LSD. Her letter clearly indicated that she did not wish to be thought of as a psychedelic artist but as a Hermetic one. While LSD could reveal glimpses of astral and etheric domains, she wrote, the process of initiation was one of gradual unfoldenment not a peak high. The experience of total freedom granted by the drug was a temporal phenomenon, inferior by comparison with the practice of evolving gradually in harmony with one's inner being.

Diana listed some of the great avatars who had inspired Western and Eastern culture, among them Christ, Buddha, Apollonius of Tyana and Lao Tse, and pointed out that their path of spiritual transformation did not require the use of hallucinogenic assistance. She went on to contrast what she felt to be the key factors differentiating the psychedelic approach from the initiatory one. Psychedelics were chemical rather than alchemical, a shock impulse rather than a catalyst for growth in the bodily matrix and only able to activate the lower regions of the Kundalini. They could also damage the etheric body rather than produce the state of internal unity symbolized by the alchemical marriage – the harmony of opposites. While psychedelics activated sexuality, the initiatory process necessarily lessened the sexual instincts gradually as one moved towards more transcendental levels of vibrancy: 'The artist passing through inner doors deep in the universal light discovers other vibrationary frequences. As an artist his work emanates from a superior level . . . .'[8]

Although Diana Vandenberg and Johfra separated in 1962, the theme of alchemical marriage has also continued in his work. Among the depictions in his Zodiac series we note that *Gemini* is surmounted by solar and lunar dragons whose necks are intertwined, while the archetypal man and woman appear to merge into a united form, mysteriously hidden from view by flames bellowing forth from the mouths of the dragons. His painting of *Libra* links the sun and moon with the symbol of infinity, and Thoth is characteristically encoiled by a caduceus consisting of a solar and lunar cobra.

His most impressive work to date is undoubtedly his *Unio Mystica*. The outer panels of the triptych contain symbols of polar unity. On the left, winged Hermes points heavenwards to the domain of the Great Mother; on the right a venerable patriarch, the Great Father or the Ancient of Days, overviews his kingdom and in particular fair Aphrodite resplendent in her sacred garden. The central panel contains a superb representation of the universal cosmic man – Adam Kadmon within the five points of a fiery pentagram. On his head is the crown of knowledge; his heart is golden mandala, his body a blaze of luminescence. Adam Kadmon rises out of the Kingdom, the archetypal fruit of the Tree of Life, reaching towards the transcendental heights of infinity and non-being.

Wilfried Satty

In the illustrations of Wilfried Satty we similarly discover a remarkable Hermetic vision of the interrelation of man and cosmos. A recurrent theme in Satty's collages is that modern technological man has narrowed his range of vision; he no longer appreciates the magnitude of the impulses which underlie the natural order and which can engulf so-called civilization in an instant. Satty's aim, in part, has been to restore that vision visually, by means of dramatically counterposed images which both frighten and evoke. Strange archetypes impinge on man's world. Mountains and forest reclaim his settlements and creations. Ancient cities merge with the landscape which has seen their ephemeral dominance for merely a brief moment in history.

Satty was born in West Germany in 1939. As a child he played with his friends in the ruins of buildings destroyed by bombs – an abandoned church tower became a kind of backyard club-house. He grew up and read the supernatural writings of Goethe and discovered the artistic vision of Grunewald and Ernst. Later he travelled through South America and Mexico observing the Meso-American pyramids and the ruins engulfed by encroaching jungle which feature so predominantly in his work. In 1965 he settled in San Francisco, and took as his studio a dark cellar in a building near the sea-front. When *McCall's* magazine decided to document the post-psychedelic occult revival on the West coast in 1970 they photographed Satty in his mysterious domain – surrounded by numerous ancient clocks, books, skulls and Buddhas. Wearing dark sunglasses and striped trousers, he was described as 'the leader of a group devoted to the study of alchemy'.

Alchemical motifs – the transmutation of man through the reintegration of the elements – are abundant in Satty's collages but the implications are wider than this. In an afterword to his illustrated edition of Ludlow's *The Hasheesh Eater*, Satty wrote: 'As above, so below. Read Paracelsus. We live in the most beautiful planet in the universe . . . .' He has called himself a 'visual alchemist', but his major theme is the reaffirmation of man's place in the cosmos.[9]

A student of Jung, Satty finds in the vestiges of ancient civilizations an overriding presence of archetypes, of guiding energies which build up cultures but which later forsake them in a process of natural cyclic growth: 'Civilizations decline, only to be replaced by others . . . communities become empires which like suns radiate their energy to the limits of their power, then decay and finally vanish, leaving behind only traces.'[10] Satty uses an assortment of images from both past and present since 'this visual vocabulary is more universal and intelligible than a verbal language and can be experienced on many levels. A tale told in such a way is timely since we live in an age when visual forms are the dominant vehicle of communications.'

Satty's graphic techniques embrace film, book and magazine illustration, silk-screen and experimental litho-offset. His illustrations have appeared in *Washington Post*, *Rolling Stone* and the *Village Voice*. He published two thematic collections of collages, *The Cosmic Bicycle* and *Time Zone*, but has also illustrated Ludlow's *The Hasheesh Eater*, Stoker's *Dracula* and more recently Edgar Allan Poe's *Tales of Mystery and Imagination*.

At a superficial glance Satty's work seems to be very much in the aftermath of earlier surrealist art. His imagery is varied and jumbled like the contents of a disturbing dream. Human and animal figures emerge from, or metamorphose into, evocative landscapes. His illustrations complement the descriptions of the hallucinatory universes of Fitz Hugh Ludlow, an early psychedelic pioneer, and the opium addict Poe.

Satty himself discounts this correlation. He notes: 'Visionary experience can be attained without drug use on a natural mind—body level. Do Hatha Yoga, take sauna, swim, eat natural foods, learn and you can share yourself with others . . . the natural understanding of the real experience in relationship to the contemporary environment can be positive.'[11]

In some ways Satty's visual representations more accurately parallel the Castaneda episodes. We find Don Juan providing Castaneda with hallucinogenic experiences in order to break down his certainty of the world and everyday senses. Later the sorcerer provides his apprentice with a more all-embracing, magical view of the world and its universal possibilities which are the domain of the shaman himself.

Satty finds common ground with the psychedelic explorers who have opened the doorway to the vast reaches of the mythological imagination but it is because they have discovered an archetypal domain. Thomas Albright, in commenting on the combination of Poe and Satty writes that Poe 'penetrated to the very core of the collective psyche, or soul, by probing into his very own . . .', and he goes on to say:[12]

> At a time when the conventions that for so long have passed as 'reality' have proven lunatic in their own way, we are perhaps less prone than before to equate the 'irrational' with madness, in which case it may be that we are now able to share Poe's visions in a spirit closer to that with which they were conceived.

Satty provides us with an evocative vision of the world which lurks close by man's own narrow perspective. Satty's procession of images tricks us out of that mesmerized certainty. In one of his illustrations to

The Hasheesh Eater a duplicated figure makes a scoffing gesture almost, as it were, in rebuking our limited perception.

Especially in his earlier work, Satty comments continually on the confusion inherent in modern society and proposes as an alternative the recognition of the universal forces which, he believes, give rise to civilizations through the passage of history.

In *Time Zone*, in one particular photo-montage we are shown a vast area of geometrically arranged 'little boxes' — a new housing development — encroaching upon wooded fields, rather like an urban cancerous disease. In another illustration nymphs stand puzzled by an iron-smelting works and elsewhere young children lie resting on a beach which further away is being quarried by industrial machinery.

Satty's emphasis however is not on a sentimental longing for the past — for a pre-industrial paradise — but on showing us how to live, how to reintegrate. As with Jung's study of archetypes and as in the magical vision of causality found in Castaneda and Western Hermeticism, the answer lies in the rediscovery of the mythological dimensions of the universe.

Satty is interested in constants — ancient cliff faces, primeval earth formations, representations of the gods who have shaped the cosmos. Gemstones are a recurring motif in his work, symbolic perhaps of the aesthetic value of the earth. Satty gives paramount importance not to vulgar metropolises which endeavour to defy nature in reaching arrogantly upwards to the sky, but to buildings like pyramids and heavy stone temples, which appear to extend out of the sand or rock on which they stand.

His cosmology entails the intermingling of the gods and man. In *Time Zone* we observe huge sculptures of the gods, which present themselves in the world as symbols of the mythological constants of mankind. One of Satty's gods derives clearly from ancient Egypt but its globe-like face suggests an outer-space connection more appropriate to the twentieth century, or beyond. An interesting illustration elsewhere in the series depicts human forms merging with trees beside the crumbling temples of a forgotten culture which is itself returning to the folds of a domineering rock formation.

Similar themes present themselves in Satty's illustrations to Edgar Allan Poe. The stories which he depicts visually are his own selection and consequently mirror his philosophy. Once again the preoccupation is with the supremacy of the forces of nature: in 'MS Found In A Bottle' a ship is battered by the ravaging currents of the ocean. In 'Ligeia' we note the imagery of a 'large, old decaying city' beside the ever-flowing Rhine. The House of Usher meanwhile is destroyed by a supernatural storm, and Satty depicts its haunting presence – the force of death which lingers until its demise – as an eerie mandala. In 'The Thousand and Second Tale of Scheherazade' Satty takes us below the level of the earth into an 'underworld' where vast caverns drip with 'myriads of gems like diamonds' and immense rivers flow 'as black as ebony and swarming with fish that have no eyes'. These are clearly allegories of the dark, unfathomed depths of the psyche.

However, Satty closes his anthology on a note of transcendental calm. Having braved the fierce and powerful vortexes of nature Satty, with Poe, settles for peaceful co-existence – a type of magical pantheism. 'Silence', 'The Conversation of Eiros and Charmion' and 'Landor's Cottage' evoke these themes, and in so doing reaffirm man's place in the manifested universe.

In 'Silence', Poe writes:[13]

> Now there are fine tales in the volumes of the Magi – glorious histories of the Heaven and of the Earth and of the mighty sea – and of the Genii that overruled the sea and the earth, and the lofty heaven. There was much love too in the sayings which were said by the Sibyls, and holy, holy things were heard of old by the dim leaves that trembled around Dodona . . . .

Satty himself is an oracle of these mysteries. Man's role is to integrate the constants of the life's expression which recur in timeless themes. In Satty's visionary art we find a procession of images which hold dramatic import for expanding our consciousness of the forces which surround us. As he himself writes: 'Man is part of nature – he must continually re-examine his role in relation to the natural experience.'[14]

Rosaleen Norton

Rosaleen Norton has a media reputation as Australia's best-known witch, but more importantly is a painter of remarkable supernatural beings. Much of her work is after the style of Norman Lindsay who was a friend and influence, and like his, her paintings have been controversial. In 1949 her works were the subject of an obscenity trial in Melbourne which she won. More recently in a quest for privacy she disappeared underground. No one seemed to know where she was living or what she was doing.

Last year with the help of a friend I tracked down a colleague of the artist's in a jeweller's shop in Sydney's Kings Cross. We explained that we wanted to discuss Rosaleen's magical techniques and influences and attempt to understand her personal view of the world, an aspect which had been considerably clouded by the somewhat brash publicity she had received in the press in earlier years.

We eventually met her. Rosaleen Norton's paintings teem with energy forms which emanate from the 'gods' of many planes and propose a supernatural, alternative reality in the tradition of Austin Spare and the Surrealists.

The artist lives by herself in a modestly furnished dwelling in a block of flats dating from the 1930s. She is wizened and frail but very much alive, with quick, darting eyes and a hearty laugh. She has dark, curly hair, and angular eyebrows which could have suggested a sinister quality were it not for her essential friendliness. In terms of their press coverage witches are not supposed to be human. They are portrayed as indulgent beings without ethics or morality or a sense of balance. Rosaleen Norton in these terms is a failure as a witch. She has kept her integrity, and interprets witchcraft in a manner quite outside ordinary conceptions.

When she was quite young, and soon after emigrating to Australia from New Zealand where she was born, she began to experience unusual shifts of perception. She would seemingly soar upwards to higher planes of being which seemed to her to be equally real, and then return to her earthly consciousness, sometimes even plunging 'below' . . . as if waking reality were only one of a series of possibilities. She says that at a very early age she became aware of the Great God Pan, the spirit of nature who has enlivened many occultists, including Aleister Crowley, Arthur Machen and Algernon Blackwood.

Pan, she felt to be a great warmth, a natural spirit of growth and vitality. She found herself lighting moss in a spontaneous attempt to burn incense out of reverence for him. And yet nothing in her background would have suggested a 'pagan' option. Her parents were practising Protestants, and were quite horrified when young Rosaleen told them of her newly found religious admiration for Pan.

When she was about twenty years of age a close friend died and Rosaleen attempted to locate her on the inner planes. She didn't quite know how to go about this, but persistent will and a desire to explore the astral worlds that she had known since early childhood prompted her on. She found the world of spirit and shadowy forms became much more real to her. It was quite definitely, she felt, an extension of the waking world and she found herself able to co-exist magically in both dimensions.

Rosaleen Norton differs from Austin Spare's magical art technique in that while he used sigils, or symbols of concentration, to unleash magical currents, she invokes the gods inwardly, and more intuitively. One occult view of the magical universe regards the supernatural domain as an extension of man's own existential reality. Rosaleen Norton rejects this hypothesis, and believes that it is a very egotistical and self-centred approach which places man on a pedestal in creation. For her the gods exist in their own right. She knows Hecate, Lucifer and Pan, not as extensions of her own consciousness, but as beings who will grace her with their presence if it pleases *them*, and not subject to her will. She says that she has discovered certain of the qualities of these gods in her own temperament and this is a natural catalyst which makes their invocation much easier and more effective. But she does not contain them in the manner of the occult practice of 'assuming the god form' for example. [15] She goes to be with them on the astral planes, and on different occasions it may be that they show different aspects or facets, of their own magical potency.

Rosaleen Norton regards Lucifer not as 'evil' so much as man's adversary. He binds and limits man when it appears that he is growing too big for his boots. He tries to trick man, not with malicious intent, so much as his exposing the limitations of the ego and man's pride in his own existence. She regards Pan as a very significant deity for the present day, a force in the universe which protects and conserves the natural beauty and resources of the environment. Pan is alive and well in the anti-pollution lobbies and among the Friends of the Earth!

Hecate on the other hand is more imposing, a frightening shadowy goddess flanked by cohorts of ghouls and night-forms, a dealer in death and a purveyor of curses. But there is a magical bond to be found here too. Rosaleen Norton sees herself as a survivor. Magic and witch-craft are her protection and inspiration in a fairly hostile, ungenerous world. Her own witchcraft has hardly brought her abundance. She lives simply, with few possessions and certainly without wealth. If she has cursed people with witch current it is a means of redressing the balance of events, a legitimate use of the magical art.

Rosaleen's paintings, as mentioned, show a certain similarity of style to those of the famous Australian decadent illustrator Norman Lindsay. Rosaleen worked as a model for Lindsay in the 1930s and 40s, and learnt much from his technique when she studied life drawing at East Sydney Technical College. But whereas for Lindsay, the world of supernature could only offer themes, for Rosaleen it was and is an ongoing reality. This is very much reflected in her work. There are fire elementals, ablaze with light; devils with dual banks of eyes, indicative of their different planes of perception; cats with magical awareness; horned beings with sensual cheeks and a strange eerie light playing on their brow. Her art is the result of the magical encounter. Energies filter through her, she says, as if she were a funnel. She transmits the current. If the gods are alive in her, her artistic medium allows them to manifest, in degrees, upon her canvas.

Rosaleen denies that she portrays the totality of the god. She can depict only those qualities the god chooses to show. The gods exist in their own right, on a plane removed from man's everyday consciousness. The role of the magician is to enlarge his consciousness to take in all these possibilities, to walk in his world knowing that it is populated by all manner of beings and entities.

In certain of Rosaleen's paintings we find creatures which are half human and half animal. These in many ways are her most convincing magical works. Although she herself is fond of satires, her paintings in this style sometimes lapse into a cartoon quality which is less impressive than her truly magical paintings.

In the works of Austin Spare, and certain of the Surrealists one gains the impression that these visionaries have become trapped and dominated by the inner destructiveness of the animal instincts, the force which the Qabalists call *Nephesch*.

For Rosaleen Norton these atavisms are in no way degraded beings. If she depicts the warlike force of Geburah on the Tree of Life as an anthropomorphic hawk, it is because within the domain of animals and birds the hawk very admirably embodies the symbolism of destructiveness and aggression. When portraying Jupiter it is fitting that the king should have lion's legs and paws because the lion is a motif of royalty, of dominance and command. The illustrations reproduced here come from a volume of Rosaleen Norton's drawings which was published in 1952 in a limited edition of one thousand copies. The drawings were in black and white and accompanied a series of poems by a talented young writer named Gavin Greenlees.

Greenlees, who is now forty-eight, is a modest and quietly spoken man for whom the magical view of the world is simultaneously a visionary and poetic expression. Like Yeats, he has been drawn to the

Tarot as a series of mystical images; he authored a series of Tarot poems, now lost, which Rosaleen Norton considers to have been among his best work.

In the published edition, Rosaleen Norton's art work appears in the context of a series of magical statements, both in terms of Greenlees's poetry, but also as an adjunct to the names of major supernatural and Qlippothic forces. It is documented with magical sources that did not become well known until the growth of interest in occult consciousness during the post-psychedelic years.

In an introduction to the book, publisher Walter Glover noted the parallels in Rosaleen Norton's art and certain of the Surrealists, although his examples of Tanguy and Matta were not, perhaps, well chosen. Glover also pointed out that her paintings embody what he called 'a vision of the night'. Rosaleen Norton had spontaneous magical experiences long before becoming acquainted with the means of structuring them through the terminology of demonology and witchcraft.

She herself has always regarded art as a medium for expressing an alternate and much more impressive reality than the dimension of normality obfuscated by human beings. In an early journal entry she wrote:[16]

> There are senses, art forms, activities and states of consciousness that have no parallel in human experience . . . an overwhelming deluge of both Universal and Self Knowledge presented (often in an allegorical form) from every conceivable aspect . . . metaphysical, mathematical, scientific, symbolic . . . . These comprise a bewildering array of experiences each complete in itself yet bearing an interblending and significant relationship to every other facet.
>
> One such experience could be compared with simultaneously watching and taking part in a play in which all art forms, such as music, drama, ceremonial ritual, shape, sound and pattern, blended into one . . . .

Rosaleen's art works are considerably varied. They range from satirical, but essentially whimsical, parodies on church figures, to Boschean whirlpools of energy forms interacting with each other, and representations of great supernatural deities.

Much of her work has been influenced by the Vorticist and Cubist schools of modern art, and if her art is at all dated, it is because of a tendency to stylization.

Her visionary images are, and continue to be, very impressive portrayals of energy spaces populated by supernatural beings.

Rosaleen's representation of Mars or Geburah – the warlike entity – for example, shows a powerful human male torso with the winged head of a hawk. The god has a scorpion's tail and clawed feet and very much embodies a sense of power and aggression. He holds a sphere in his right hand which could almost be the puny globe of Earth, under his influence.

Her portrait of Jupiter shows a proud potentate with a resplendent light issuing from his forehead, and a dark, majestic beard lapping down on to his chest. His legs and tail are leonine, and he carries in his right hand the mace of authority.

In both of these pictures, Rosaleen Norton depicts her deities as an animal–human fusion, rather as Austin Spare did in much of his work. For her, animals characterize a dignity that man has lost. She is especially fond of cats because of their 'psychic qualities', and the lion therefore becomes an appropriate symbolic aspect of one of the major rulers of the magical universe.

Rosaleen says in many ways she feels that the animal kingdom has retained its integrity to a far greater extent than the human. She is one with animals, for whom she feels a natural empathy. Many human beings, however, she despises for their narrow world-view. Cats, she believes, operate in waking consciousness and on the astral plane simultaneously.

She recalls what she feels may have been a previous incarnation. She lived in a past century in a rickety wooden house in a field of yellow grass near Beachy Head in Sussex. There were animals – cows, horses and so on – and she was a poltergeist. She remembers understanding the techniques by which poltergeists make objects move. And yet when 'real' people came near her house they were offended and frightened by her presence. They could not relate to her poltergeist condition, and she in turn found herself attacking them out of contempt. The animals however were no trouble at all. They regarded her as another cohabitant, as part of the 'natural order'.

Her love of animals and her antipathy towards much of what the human race has come to represent has of course influenced her magical conceptions. And yet she acknowledges duelling factions within the animal kingdom as representing important themes of 'polarity'.

The hawk, for example, is a natural predator, and is a fitting representation of the Martian archetype. Her preference for animals is thus clearly not an escape into the non-human. On the contrary the animal kingdom contains a range of activities and functions from which mankind has much to learn.

The necessity for a sense of balance shows itself well in another of her pictures, *Esoteric Study*. An angry demon leers across from the Qlippothic realm, counter-balanced by a diamond shape of white radiance on the other side. The scales are issuing out of the cosmic egg, and the superimposition of the magician's face on the scales themselves suggests that she is the vehicle through which all the tides of energy flow, asserting their polarities of balance accordingly.

Gavin Greenlees's accompanying poem begins:

> Out of herself, the Earth created by her own guardian faces,
> And using the rule they gave her, out of herself
> She made creatures to serve her, – animals, poems,
> Forgotten beings, men, women . . . . Out of herself
> She made the grandeur and its faith, healthy or faded . . . .

One of Rosaleen Norton's most impressive portraits is titled *Individuation*. She has denied a direct influence from the Tarot, regarding it more as an intuitive source than as a series of meditative doorways to inner states. Nevertheless, in several respects we find here a parallel with the card *Temperance*. The figure depicted is a fusion of the animal, the human and the divine:

> I speak the birth,
> I speak the beginning of presence
> I am inauguration, I am a greeting between friends
> One flower, one animal, one phrase,
> One illusion, one discovering in one world!

The figure stands astride the Zodiac drawn down into a mountain of forms, yet rising transcendent above them. The genius is both male and female, indicative of the hermaphroditic qualities of the Qabalistic 'Middle Pillar'. The drawing follows *Panic*, which closely resembles *The Tower*, the card in the Tarot which counterposes Temperance on the Tree and provides a symbolic warning of the forceful energy levels of higher states.

Rosaleen Norton's tower is exceptionally organic and phallic, again indicative of the reproductive, Nephesch quality in witchcraft, and the genital region on the Tree of Man. It is surmounted by the Horned God – horns symbolizing for her the dual polarities of magical energy. A cascade of liquid energy courses around the column, and in the bottom of her picture we notice a hand outpouring a wave of astral forms. We are reminded also of the Eastern parallels with this drawing, in the form of the Kundalini energy arousal in sexual, tantric yoga.

If this drawing is austere and forbidding, like its Tarot equivalent it can be regarded as a pathway to a higher state of integration in the psyche, and this follows, significantly, with *Individuation* – a reference to Jung's term for inner wholeness.

Rosaleen Norton conceives of totality as a fusion of magical polarities and her artistic imagery unquestionably shares more common ground with the Gnostic Abraxas principle of good and evil reconciled in one form, and Aleister Crowley's Thoth pack, than with the more decorative Pre-Raphaelite style of the Waite/Coleman Tarot cards.

If *Individuation* depicts integration of forms, its predecessor *Panic* shows the magician's confrontation with his own identity – the question of his ego and pride of place in a universe which frequently mocks his aspirations.

Greenlees writes:

> Amid dreams, he saw the high Oneiric horned column,
> the idiot eye,
> the tusky trumpets,
> Soundless of Tiamaat, horror of vacancy, the uneasy
> museum with its dead music . . . .
>
> So amid the silent mountains once, we others having gone ahead,
> – we heard your voice calling . . . .

Rosaleen Norton's expression of her magical universe has not always attracted a receptive audience. During the period of obscenity accusations levelled at her work, a large part of the limited edition was destroyed by customs police. Had Austin Spare, whose occult paintings often show dancing naked witches and other supernatural entities, lived in Australia at this time, his work would have suffered a similar fate. We are reminded also that Norman Lindsay's paintings, now popular within the context of the current preference for nostalgia, were for many years considered to be thoroughly indecent. His so-called 'pagan works' and Rosaleen Norton's pantheistic forms are permissible in the context of 'mythology' but are frowned upon when they acquire the status of a possible alternative reality.

In the present day, while Lindsay's work is now widely known, Rosaleen Norton has been neglected and forgotten. Austin Spare suffered a similar fate. Sargeant thought him brilliant, but when Spare began to illustrate his own magical concepts in privately produced books, he took himself outside the domain where artistic careers are made.

Much the same has occurred with Rosaleen Norton. The public recalls her status as a witch, with its unbecoming connotations, but forgets her significance as a magical artist.

Rosaleen Norton is both familiar with, and to some extent a part of, the Golden Dawn system of magic. She admires Yeats for his poetic genius and MacGregor Mathers for his skill in interpreting mythology. Crowley's poem, 'Hymn to Pan', she regards as a fine work, but she dismisses his art as poor, and dislikes what she feels was his cruel regard for animals.

Rosaleen Norton is clearly no mere 'witch'. She operates in a universal domain, teaming with magical beings of varying attributes and qualities. In this sense she espouses a similar world-view to that of Carlos Castaneda's *brujo*, Don Juan, with whom she is personally unfamiliar. The magician, as a magician, has different responses to causality from those dictated by the scientific, empirical tradition. It is required that he open himself to an infinite range of possibility. He must learn to dwell with supernatural entities on their own terms.

The rise of cosmic music

The Beginnings

The psychedelic period has been characterized by some as a time of considerable unrest and unreality. We recall the youth of the United States during this time – rebellious on the political front, outraged by Vietnam and seemingly willing to embrace any form of 'escapist' mysticism which offered not only a demonstration of the validity of one's identity but a direction towards the ground of all 'Being'. Zen, Yoga, Buddhism, meditation, magic and Tarot were all intertwined in these years during the beginning of what has now become a less spectacular, if more sober 'consciousness' movement. It is now possible to look back almost academically in retrospect, and discern in the early craving for spirituality, the first evidence of a shamanistic intent in modern society, the first signs in the present era of man demanding renewed contact with the sacred.

The music of the time – and I am referring to the popular contemporary music which was actually at the base of this shift in consciousness – reflected the changing direction of the young people of the 1960s.

One of the most influential West Coast groups on the 'acid' scene was Country Joe and the Fish. Their album *I Feel Like I'm Fixin to Die* today seems naive and even trivial. It featured parodies on America's war effort but was also part of the quest for an identity:[1]

> Who am I . . . to stand and wander, to wait,
> While the Wheel of Fate slowly grinds my life away . . . .

However, within the mystical undercurrent of the counter-culture – whose music was finally to emerge in one form as cosmic rock – there was a new preoccupation with mythological and religious themes.

Steppenwolf, who took their name from Hermann Hesse's famous novel, displayed in their lyric to 'Spiritual Fantasy' a kind of

theosophical eclecticism. Society would be saved by spiritual masters
who could discern beneath the fabric of existence, an underriding
unity – a Oneness of Creation:[2]

> Humanity grew weary of its state of mind,
> So it summoned from far and it called from near,
> All the wise men for to be sincere,
> To heal its wounds, and make it whole,
> And lead the way back to the soul
> . . . the wise men came together
> And they found that all the teachings were the same.

The Scottish hippy folk group, The Incredible String Band, who
were especially popular in the United States and whose music was a
happy rambling pot-pourri of ideas and enthusiasms, similarly explored
mystical concepts like reality, illusion and reincarnation – particularly
in their Eastern context, although they later turned to Scientology.

'Big Ted', the story of a reincarnated pig, is especially humorous but
also includes the prevalent idea that all beings are responsible for their
own destiny:

> Ted may be a bull cow next time around . . . .
> He'll be whatever he will choose on air or sea or ground.

The Incredible String Band went on to pose questions similar to those
of Country Joe and the Fish concerning identity:[3]

> Maya, Maya . . . all this world is but a play . . .
> Be thou the joyful player . . . .

But their vision was already expanding to a folk-interpretation of the
Creation process.

On their *Wild Horses* album a major song entitled 'Creation' describes
seven mythological days of awakening:[4]

> The first day was golden,
> And she coloured the sun
> And she named it Hyperion
> And she made it a day of light and healing
> The second day was silver,
> And she coloured the moon,
> And she named it Phoebe,
> And she made a day of enchantment and the living waters . . . .

These lyrics parallel the poetry of the Tarot with its mythological associations.

Welsh folk singer Donovan meanwhile went on to literalize the mythic process by combining quasi-anthropology and fantasy in his song 'Atlantis', a million seller. In a manner which predated Eric Von Daniken he described the ante-diluvian kings of Atlantis as colonizers of the world:[5]

> All the gods who play in the mythological dramas in all
> legends from all lands, came from Atlantis . . . .

The sources we have been describing were part of the late 1960s concern for an all-embracing mythological or spiritual reality. However, one factor which emerges quite clearly is that these singers – spokesmen of their time – were still weavers of *themes*. There is not yet in their work the sense that the music should literally transform its audience. This was to come later with the discarding of the lyric and its replacement by the mantra – in the form of the electronic, mind-altering textures of the moog synthesizer.

The preoccupation with mystical themes continued nevertheless – and is still present in much of the more recent outpourings. While Mick Jagger chose to impersonate a Dionysian Satan on stage and describe the Devil's presence through history in the lyrics of 'Sympathy with the Devil',[6] David Bowie in his song 'Quicksand' made specific mention of the Golden Dawn magical society:[7]

> I'm closer to the Golden Dawn,
> Immersed in Crowley's uniform of imagery,
> I'm torn between the light and dark,
> Where others see their target, divine symmetry.

Another British rock group which drew heavily on white magic sources for its lyrical content was that headed by the late Graham Bond. Bond was characteristic of the gravelly voiced rock singer who had found his niche in the standard 12-bar format of the blues. He did not easily transform to mystical sublimity, but nevertheless titled his first album *Holy Magick*[8] – a reference to Aleister Crowley's special spelling with a 'k'. The album contained details of the Qabalistic Cross – a magical exercise for raising one's spiritual energy force through various 'chakra' levels. A later release, *We Put Our Magick On You*[9] contained titles like 'Moving Towards The Light', 'Druid' and

115

'Hail Ra Herakhite', the latter being the Egyptian form of Horus with whom Crowley especially identified.

Occult and mystical themes seem to have exercised a surprising influence on pop lyrics since the late 1960s – even in cases where the performer was operating in a musical medium quite removed from the more free-form frameworks of music, as found in the raga, for example.

Folk singer Judee Sill, from Oakland, California, created a sensation in the United States with her initial offering – which included a strong dose of alchemical and apocalyptic mysticism served up through a drawling Southern accent.[10] Bob Dylan's backing group The Band meanwhile combined some fine country rock music with lyrics which embraced not only confederate history and faded sepia memories of Southern living, but also references to magic:[11]

> I do believe in your hexagram
> . . . but can you tell me how they all move the Plan . . .?

Pete Sinfield, a poet formerly attached to the British group King Crimson whom we shall consider presently – has more recently drawn on reincarnational ideas in his lyrics:[12]

> Still I wonder if I passed some time ago
> As a bird or stream, or tree . . .
> To mount up high you first must sink down low . . . .

The themes of rebirth, renewed spiritual awareness, the oneness of Creation have continued to the present time. But while this eclectic mix of mystical images was itself born of the counter-culture interest in these areas it was from the more electronic side of its musical expression that the most far-reaching changes have come.

I have neglected in my treatment above to stress that apart from the mellow, introspected folk lyricism which was indeed a central part of the music of the 'new consciousness' there was also the aggressive music of performers like Jimi Hendrix which above all else was an expression of rage and intensity. Hendrix played his guitar strings with his teeth. His voice was lost in currents of electronic feedback. His fierce rendition of 'Star Spangled Banner' before the Woodstock crowd – the largest concert audience in history – was an indictment of his country's hawkish identity.[13]

But Hendrix and his fellow collaborators in acid rock – music specifically designed to be heard under drug influence – were laying a new basis. Theirs was the foundation of what would later become the music of cosmic textures. Acid rock, elastic, mind-expanding, was an – albeit primitive – assault on the senses. It demanded a response of its audience. It was also the first music designed specifically for ear-phones – the beginning of the private, inner voyage.

In one of his most famous performances Hendrix asked: 'Are you *really* experienced?', and it was to be this factor which would really distinguish such music from the more thematic approach. Relating themes is a far cry from embodying them.

Inner-Space connections – enter Pink Floyd

In England, the avant-garde rock group Pink Floyd laid the ground for a new refinement which grew out of acid rock and which was – in the Hendrix sense – experimental. Their music was not just electronic, it was cosmic. And as such it was the first blossoming flower of a new magical form – the music of transformation.

A new theme emerged – the parallel between inner and outer space. In the film *2001* Stanley Kubrick had already made some of these connections in aligning astrological and rebirth themes with the astronomical voyage, and the soundtrack featured evocative, electronic voices.[14] Pink Floyd's early work was characterized by compositions like 'Astronomy Domine' and 'Set the Controls for the Heart of the Sun' – and there were some mythological connections too, in works like 'Sysyphus' for example.[15] Pink Floyd were still entranced by the novelty of psychedelia – witness the flurry of animal screeches and effects on 'Several species of Small Furry Animals' but their cosmic, electronic music had an eerie loneliness – emblematic of a new and untried area of enlarged consciousness. But they never quite allowed their paths of entry to take them too far from reality. Usually humour or flippancy intruded. When Roger Waters of Pink Floyd combined with Ron Geesin to write the soundtrack for a film based on a journey through man's alimentary canal – a fundamentalist equivalent of the search for inner man – they titled their songs in a bizarre, comical fashion: 'Dance of the Red Corpuscles' – 'Embryonic Womb-Walk' and so on.[16]

It was only with their master work *Meddle* that the full impact of their music made itself felt. The exquisite instrumental 'Echoes' conjures up pearls of water, vibrations through crystalline space. A superbly developed composition, it closes with a soaring, uplifting movement which seem to imply a transformation of plane – an astral journey to another dimension.[17]

Their next major album, *The Dark Side of the Moon*, was more notable for its lyrics than its textural, evocative qualities. 'Brain Damage' – a curious song of lunacy, reminiscent of R. D. Laing's writings, perhaps revealingly pointed to Pink Floyd's unwillingness to push their cosmic entry too far:[18]

> And if the dam breaks open many years too soon,
> And if there is no room upon the hill,
> And if your hand explores with dark forbodings too
> I'll see you on the dark side of the moon.

Pink Floyd's next offering was similarly hesitant. Again their lyrics revealed an incipient paranoia: In 'Shine On You Crazy Diamond': Roger Waters wrote:

> Now there's a look in your eyes, like black holes in the sky . . .
> you reached for the secret too soon . . .; you cried for the moon
> – threatened by shadows at night and exposed in the light

'Wish You Were Here' includes the quixotic lines:[19]

> So you think you can tell Heaven from Hell, blue skies from pain
> Can you tell a green field from a cold steel rail.
> A smile from a veil. . . .
> And did they get you to trade your heroes for ghosts . . .?

The album was interestingly packaged, however, to include representation on its cover of each of the four elements – air, water, fire and earth. Each had a surreal torch. A 'bodiless' executive (clothes only) astride in the desert sands – human legs pointing vertically out of a placid lake – a man with his clothes on fire and so on.

In Britain Pink Floyd were not the only electronic musicians to combine inner–outer space themes. A group called Hawkwind worked with well-known science-fiction author Michael Moorcock to produce the *Space Ritual*, an outer space-occult mix,[20] and Yes recorded several grandiose, electronic albums featuring the space-art of Roger Dean on their covers.[21] Their music was somewhat more abrasive, and less evocative than Pink Floyd's and suffered from self-conscious over-embellishment. There were some interesting developments though. The first British album to combine tarot card imagery with electronic textures was released in 1975 by Steve Hackett. Titled *Voyage of the*

Acolyte,[22] it contained an impressive range of instrumentation including mellotron, harmonium, flute, synthesizer, bells, vibraphone, oboe and cello in addition to the more orthodox instruments. Only certain Tarot cards were chosen: The Ace of Wands, The High Priestess, The Tower, The Lovers, The Hermit and The Hierophant.

Hackett's lyric for The Hermit recalls his familiar representation in the A. E. Waite Rider-Pack:

> Enshrouded by darkness,
> A figure slowly forms,
> Through many years of banishment
> No shelter from the storm
> To find this slave of solitude
> You'll know him by his star . . . .

The consciousness state symbolized by this card is the mystical Dark Night of the Soul – the plunge into the profound but isolating inner blackness which approaches the 'anonymous' quality of the Void.

Meanwhile, another experimental group, King Crimson, announced to its concert audiences that its music was a form of 'white magic'. Until its recent disbandonment its mainstay and spokesman was Robert Fripp, a complex, elusive character who peered down on his audience through metal spectacles and who believed in the visionary quality of his group's music. Fripp is a student of the Qabalah, Wicca, the Bhagavad Gita and Paracelsus – he has certainly mixed his sources. Much of King Crimson's early music was orthodox, but evocative, full bodied rock music with a mellotron base. Gradually it expanded so that on a late album, *Islands*,[23] there were both electronic, textural innovations and a composition distinctly reminiscent of Vivaldi. This wide range of styles gave King Crimson impact through unpredictability. Fripp has said in interviews that music can reach out through complexity to provide a sonic, healing effect as it permeates its audience. 'It is a very important tool in that if you can bring everybody together on one vibration you can create a oneness and an energy without parallel. Playing before an audience is a magical rite.'[24] Fripp was perhaps the first contemporary musician to express a consciously felt desire to transform his listeners – and this is characteristic of what I have called the experiential domain of the more recent cosmic rock music. It has outgrown its former themes and has replaced them as it were with the alternative reality itself. Fripp called it 'the union of mind and soul in an exploding revelation, the polarity of the divine Consciousness in material form'.

Other guitarists have of course explored meditative frameworks. Carlos Santana and John McLaughlin have both embraced the spiritual philosophy of Sri Chinmoy, but Fripp is perhaps less devotional and more demonstrative in his attitudes.

His most recent work, with synthesizer musician Brian Eno, has moved towards a new refinement – away from effect and into the purity of essence. *Evening Star*[25] is a remarkable statement of this newly found simplicity. Even its composition titles demonstrate an integration of the elements: 'Wind or Water', 'Wind or Wind' and 'An Index of Metals' – with its hint of alchemy.

While other musicians have had impact, Pink Floyd and King Crimson have been foremost in Britain in terms of their impact on the 'new consciousness'.

For reasons of space, we have omitted several prominent groups from our discussion – Jade Warrior, Emerson, Lake and Palmer, The Alan Parson's Project – who recorded an electronic rendition of 'The Mystery Tales of Edgar Allan Poe' – and Mike Oldfield whose space music was used in the film *The Exorcist*. But my essential aim is to show a correlation between the new directions in contemporary pop and electronic music and the various, and many, means of approaching inner-space levels of awareness.

European developments – transcending the lyric

There is no doubt that the most evocative and far-reaching explorations in what we may term 'cosmic music', have taken place on the Continent. The key figures are a remarkably tight-knit group of German musicians linked to the Ohr, Brain, Metronome and Virgin labels. Tangerine Dream, Ash Ra Tempel and, in a solo capacity, Edgar Froese and Klaus Schulze, were influenced by Pink Floyd during their formative beginnings, but their music has these days grown totally beyond the frameworks of lyrical expression.

Progressive rock music on the Continent passed through the same 'astronomical' orientation as Pink Floyd. Italian group Le Orme worked with English writer Peter Hammill to produce *Felona and Sorona*[26] – a concept album based on the mythical dualism of two sister planets in distant outer space – each unaware of each other or of their organic relation to the manifested universe. The German three-man outfit Dzyan (named after the ancient pre-Vedic book annotated by Madame Blavatsky) have similarly produced an avant-garde album with compositions like 'Light Shining out of Darkness', 'Magika' and 'Time Machine'.[27]

Tangerine Dream's earlier electronic albums for the Ohr label featured impressive abstract outer space landscapes on their covers, and bore evocative titles like *Zeit*, *Alpha Centauri* and *Atem*. Their compositions were given titles such as 'Sunrise in the third system', 'Birth of liquid pleides', 'Origin of supernatural probabilities'. Again their music had the same haunting, eerie loneliness as early Pink Floyd. It was sugges- tive of: vibrations in space – the music of cosmic processes – the essential smallness of man – the grandeur of the manifested universe in the sea of infinite creation.

German cosmic rock is an electronic metamorphosis from the more primitive, psychedelic acid rock. Early on, the innovative Ash Ra Tempel performed live with Timothy Leary and their keyboards specialist Klaus Schulze has since emerged, with Tangerine Dream's Edgar Froese, as the leading exponent of cosmic texture music.

Tangerine Dream were until recently a group of three – Froese, Peter Baumann and Christoph Franke. The band formed in 1965 and at first played conventional rock music in the Anglo-American tradition. In 1967 however they became caught up in the experimental musical vortex forming in Berlin. They discarded drums and turned to complex and technologically advanced electronic synthesizers. They listened to Pink Floyd, but also to Liszt, Debussy, Wagner, Stockhausen and Ligeti. They grappled – as Robert Fripp was to later – with the concept of transformation – and the musical effects on the recipient audience.

Their first albums released in Germany between 1970 and 1972 reached only a limited European audience. In 1974 however Tangerine Dream signed with the English Virgin label and produced an electronic album of considerable beauty and dignity. *Phaedra* – named after the doomed daughter of King Minos of Crete – opens with a passage resembling the richness of Peer Gynt. It explores silken textures and ethereal forms in an extraordinary undulating manner. The group began to tour England and, instead of playing only in concert halls and auditoriums, were able to perform within the more tranquil confines of York Minster and Coventry and Liverpool Cathedrals – the sacred places. This seems to me to be a very significant feature of their music – its endeavour to explore mystical spaces and make them manifest on sanctified ground. The group played to their audiences in total darkness to enhance the effect of their music.

In Germany itself the growth of cosmic music has been a widespread phenomenon involving a larger spectrum of musicians. The groups have colourful and bizarre names – Annexus Quam, Epsylon, Nektar, Wallenstein, Guru Guru, Mythos and the Cosmic Jokers. The medium has predictably drawn forth both strongly commercial and also more avant-garde elements. It could be said with some justification that an organization calling itself the Cosmic Couriers has been guilty of marketing oversell, using as some of its catch phrases 'Music forms our dreams' and 'our melodies fly through the spheres'. The operation began in 1973 as a music complex geared to linking electronic music and science fiction. While sound engineer Dieter Dierks buried himself in a quadrophonic studio in order to come up with a new transcendental electronic formula, the marketing had already begun: 'Adventures wait for us. Unlimited fantasy. This is Sci Fi. The Science Fiction of Pleasure. It comes in the magic of colours, in the flashes of light, in the sounds of the electrons' . . . . With it came new trends in Sci-Fi clothing, new magazines, new toys.

But while the concept of Rolf-Ulrich Kaiser's Cosmic Couriers was obviously a promotional image (one of the more blatant album releases being named *Galactic Supermarket!*), certain of the individual musicians were able to rise above the commercial flurry.

Klaus Schulze, the keyboards member of the original Ash Ra Tempel has extensively influenced the direction of what we have termed 'cosmic music'. His individual works, *Cyborg, Blackdance, Moondawn,* and *Mirage* especially, incorporate the evocative textural qualities found in the music of Tangerine Dream. On *Blackdance*, Schulze merged synthesizer with gentle acoustic guitar. His own sustained rhythms were muted, mysterious and dignified – taking on the qualities of a mantra. Ernst Walter Siemon's bass chanting was reminiscent of the soloist in a Russian Orthodox Choir.[28] *Cyborg* saw Schulze interposing his synthesizer with cello to produce an effect suggestive of melancholic isolation on a distant planet.

Schulze's colleague Manuel Gottsching meanwhile has recently been exploring quadrophonic permutations of the electric guitar. On his *Inventions* album[29] he explored basic, primal musical patterns, again in the mantric repetitive style, but with an emergent, expansive quality. 'Quasarsphere' is a fine work built on mutations in texture, musical colours flowing into themselves.

An implicit mystical direction is also found in the *Meditation Mass* of Yatha Sidra.[30] This is an eclectic mix – Rolf and Klaus Richter combined moog synthesizer, Indian flute, vibraphone and electric piano for the four-part composition. Peter Elbracht's excellent, reflective passages of flute playing are comparable in style to Paul Horn's poetic flute paean recorded within the dome of the Taj Mahal: one of the outstanding mystical albums of the 1960s.[31]

Among the most interesting manifestations of the cosmic rock style was Walter Wegmuller's work *Tarot*.[32] More advanced conceptually than Steve Hackett's *Voyage of the Acolyte*, Wegmuller's double album attempted musically to chart the various inner spaces appropriate to each of the Tarot Major Arcana. He used several prominent musicians, among them Schulze and Gottsching, but also Jurgen Dollase, another influential performer. Included with the boxed records, Wegmuller provided a set of imaginative stylized Tarot reproductions.

While Wegmuller's lyrics are in German and at times dominate the more abstract qualities of the accompaniment, the album characterizes what seems to me to be the dominant aspect of this musical style – the merging of electronically based textures with an awareness of the inner symbolic domain of the mind itself. While the concept album *Tarot* explored the common ground between music and magical consciousness, a significant but isolated approach linking mythology and electronic music had already come forth from Sweden.

In 1971 a keyboards musician named Bo Hansson rented a house on an island near Stockholm with the express purpose of recording some music inspired directly by Tolkien's *Lord of the Rings*. Hansson was aware of Tolkien's impact in England but what is of interest to us is that he wished to record a space-rock interpretation of a mythological cycle. We recall that W. Y. Evans-Wentz, the American scholar who translated *The Tibetan Book of the Dead* into English wrote his Ph.D thesis for the University of Rennes on the mythology of fairies and goblins. In this work, first published in 1911 as *The Fairy-Faith in Celtic Countries* he compiled statements of belief concerning fairy creatures from country folk in Brittany, Ireland, Wales, the Isle of Man and Cornwall.[33] Evans-Wentz's view was that the fairy-faith reflected an intuitive perception of another level of consciousness – in other words that fairies, demons, angels, gnomes, goblins and elementals were all symbolic *of states of mind*.

Bo Hansson's music now acquires a more special significance. Like the Pink Floyd/Tangerine Dream development from psychedelic rock, Hansson had himself been directly influenced by Jimi Hendrix, and the two toured together in Scandinavia in the mid-1960s. We have described the inner space development as a direct musical expression of the directions towards a transcendental reality – for Hansson, Tolkien's mythical cycle plumbed depths of the imagination appropriate to his own environment. Scandinavia is rich in folk legends of spirit beings and Hansson endeavoured to record his music directly as a result of the moods conjured up by Tolkien's writings. He himself was unable to write music, and so his album – an evocative blend of electronic effects, saxophone and flute – consisted of direct musical impressions. Particularly effective were 'Fog on the Barrow Downs' – with its gentle misty sequences and guitar notes reminiscent of wolves – and 'Journey to Dark' which conjured up the hints of evil found in *Lord of the Rings*.[34]

Hansson, Tangerine Dream and Klaus Schulze especially have taken their music into transcendental spaces which thoroughly complement the expansive directions inherent in the 'new consciousness'.

Significantly the abstract, textural mode itself is well suited to both meditative and magical practice. It becomes possible to overlay the mantras of Yoga and the Qabalistic intonations appropriate to the Sephirothic spheres on the Tree of Life. Edgar Froese's *Aqua* for example, as its title suggests, is a quadrophonic exploration of the textural implications of the water element.[35] Robert Fripp and Brian Eno's *Evening Star* has an exquisite uplifting effect which constitutes a musical complement to the contemplative, rebirth state of mind. Pink Floyd's 'Echoes' is an admirable adjunct to any attempt to project into astral, out-of-the-body consciousness . . . and so on. 'Inner space' music is primarily important because of its commitment to exploring sensory and tactile inputs, twisting our awareness, evoking images.

In its finest and purest form, it is music that John Lilly – if he hasn't heard it already – could very well take with him into his meditation tank.

CONCLUSION

Where is it all going?

As we have seen, one of the major thrusts of the counter-culture at present is the search for an expressive mythology. The eclecticism which underlies the renewed interest in altered states of consciousness encompasses the cosmologies of *The Tibetan Book of the Dead*, the *I Ching*, the yoga of Patanjali, the Qabalah, the Tarot and Celtic traditions. There is no doubt that in merging with popular culture the conceptual base of these philosophies has become intermingled with more recent ideas and, as Gershom Scholem would have it, a process of unscholarly fusion has taken place. The exotic art of Abdul Mati Klarwein, with its flurry of Qabalistic and Tantric motifs, finds its way onto jazz and rock album covers; the fantasy domain of Roger Dean, embracing medieval castles, hybrid monsters and bizarre machines, embellishes posters, books and T shirts. Our visual mania has allowed us to bring our mythological impulses into the tangible world of the everyday.

It would be easy enough to dismiss the present trends of the counter-culture if it were not for the fact that its cumulative direction does seem to point to a deeply felt need for belief systems which allow a sense of identification with the earth, the environment and the forces of nature. The counter-culture is founded on alternative modes of thought and demands a meaningful approach to the earth's resources both in terms of the physical terrain and the creative, transformative aspects of consciousness.

The new approaches in transpersonal psychology have brought a new-found relationship between physiological and biological aspects of the human organism, and transcendental states of mind, so that it is now meaningful to examine religious and metaphysical systems in terms of the potential for growth which they offer. Robert Masters and Jean Houston, through their 'mind games' have offered a tangible means of exploring altered states of awareness, and developing the sensory imagination, by methods which owe their essential structure to a mythological view of the world. The descent into the unconscious takes on all the ramifications of the shaman's journey into the night-time of ancestral images, where in less sophisticated societies than ours, sacred meaning as a basis for living has long been discerned.

Jung pointed to the significance of archetypal imagery as a vital component of mental health, in establishing the basis of modern analytical psychology. John Lilly has since proposed that the range of consciousness opened up by the meditative encounter with symbolic images is also a crucial factor. Our only limits are limits of belief, for the most profound programmes of mystical awareness in the human biocomputer are open-ended and totally awesome.

In the Tarot we have one example of a contemporary shamanistic framework for entering those regions of the creative imagination which have enlivened visionary forms of art and music. And it is significant that the new directions towards 'alternative realities' do not constitute an escape from the world as has often been claimed in criticism of the counter-culture, so much as a reaffirmation of those vital processes which are most meaningful in retaining the faculties of creativity and growth.

Charles Tart's distinction of 'state-specific sciences' may well be the turning point both for new inroads of research into the potential of the mind, and also for an understanding of the essential relativity of the scientific method. In acknowledging that scientism is a world-view like any other, we have begun to examine the nature of belief, the models and paradigms used in formulating laws of causality, and most important of all, the levels of consciousness which underlie advances in perception and understanding. The fact that the mode of consciousness which an investigator finds himself in determines the fruits of his analysis has been well made by those who have stressed that our science, language and everyday communication is based on a consensus reality.

At present the art and music of the counter-culture, with its fusion of mythological and symbolic themes, indicates a new willingness to explore faculties of creativity which open inroads to states of consciousness outside previously defined boundaries. It comes as little surprise that the essentially anarchistic Dadaist exhibitions of the 1920s attracted such a strong emotional reaction in some quarters that it was necessary for police to be called in to close them to public display. Dadaism and Surrealism provide a totally new vision of the world, an extension of agreed-upon limits of perceptual reality. The new visionary art of Roger Dean, Abdul Mati Klarwein, Bill Martin, Ernst Fuchs, and others, builds upon a similar premise. We are once again host to a fusion of the familiar and the transcendent. Everyday images and mythological concepts are given equal ground in the works of these painters. And meanwhile, ironically enough, the archetypes are beginning to encroach on the consensus consciousness by means of the commercial machine which has developed to exploit the needs of the youth culture.

In this book I have considered varying sources of the new mythology, some of which may have seemed less important than others. We might agree, for example, that the Tarot in the shamanistic sense does include a range of archetypal motifs which in turn make their appearance in visionary forms of art. But does this sensibility also extend to the admittedly transient nature of contemporary popular music? My feeling is that, at the present time, it does. Since the 1960s contemporary music has seen remarkable shifts of ground embracing the folk rock of Bob Dylan, the aggressive blues-based rock music of the Rolling Stones, new exploratory fusions in jazz and electronic music. Those who were present during the years of change which saw a revival of meaning in the *I Ching*, Buddhism, Yoga and the Tarot, and who at present constitute a large proportion of the ongoing and transformative counter-culture, have gravitated towards musical forms which reflect these shifts of consciousness. It is no accident that the German school of cosmic music has developed from earlier and more bombastic forms of tactile 'acid-rock' music. But the significant factors are the new components: Bo Hansson's mythological—electronic mix, Tangerine Dream's performances in the sacred domain of the cathedral, Robert Fripp's awareness of textural, mantric music as a mind-elevating medium of expression.

We are living in interesting times – an era in fact which may well see major transformations in the consensus reality. Physical considerations such as world energy shortages and a new-found respect for environmental cycles are perhaps the ground basis for a new ecology of the mind. The emergence of a far-ranging and eclectic cosmology to mirror these shifts in the everyday world-view will not be far behind.

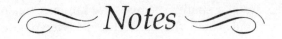# Notes

Introduction: Counter-culture, magic and the new consciousness

1 P. Fry and M. Long, *Beyond the Mechanical Mind*, p.12.
2 See *The Occult*, a special report of the Anglican Commission of Enquiry, headed by Archbishop Marcus Loane, Sydney, 1975.
3 C. Tart, *Altered States of Consciousness*, p.291 et seq.

Chapter 1: The magical universe

1 The accounts of Carlos Castaneda have recently been questioned by Richard de Mille in *Castaneda's Journey* (1976), but at the time of writing Castaneda had not responded to de Mille's charge that don Juan was an imaginary concoction. There seems to be general agreement that the themes of Castaneda's books are authentic, whether or not they are borrowed from other anthropological sources.
2 See R. Hughes, *Heaven and Hell in Western Art*, p.22.
3 G. Chevalier, *The Sacred Magician*, p.95.
4 Ibid., p. 96.
5 F. Bardon, *The Practice of Magical Evocation*, p.59.
6 Ibid., p.125.
7 Ibid., p.126.
8 Ibid., p.19.
9 See Edward F. Heenan, *Mystery, Magic and Miracle*, p. 85, and I. Zaretsky and M. Leone, *Religious Movements in Contemporary America*, P. 663.
10 S. Arieti, *Creativity*, p.221.
11 *777* is included in A. Crowley, *The Qabalah of Aleister Crowley*, an anthology of major magical writings.
12 A. Crowley, *The Qabalah of Aleister Crowly*, introduction by Israel Regardie.
13 G. Scholem, *Kabbalah*, p.203.
14 H. Zimmer, *The King and the Corpse*, p.178.

Chapter 2: Archetypes and belief systems

1 C. G. Jung, *The Integration of the Personality*, p.89.
2 I. Regardie, *The Art and Meaning of Magic*, p.13.
3 C. G. Jung, 'The Structure of the Psyche' in *The Structure and Dynamics of the Psyche*, p.158.

4 W. E. Butler, *Magic, its Ritual Power and Purpose*, pp.17-18.
5 J. Jacobi, *The Psychology of C. G. Jung*, pp.47-48.
6 E. Edinger, *Ego and Archetype*, p.96.
7 W. E. Butler, op.cit., p.16.
8 D. Fortune, *The Mystical Qabalah*, pp.10-11.
9 J. Jacobi, op.cit., p.94.
10 Ibid., p.139.
11 Ibid., p.152.
12 See especially E. Howe, *The Magicians of the Golden Dawn*, referred to in Chapter 1.
13 J. Lilly, *Simulations of God*, p.84.
14 See especially M. Eliade, *Cosmos and History*.
15 J. Lilly, op.cit., pp.146-7.
16 See M. Eliade, *Shamanism*, p.42.
17 S. Arieti, *Creativity*.
18 J. Lilly, *The Dyadic Cyclone*, Chapter 12.

Chapter 3: The Tarot and transformation

1 This concept is an integral part of modern magical thought and is central to the definitions of magic proposed by Dion Fortune and Aleister Crowley.
2 For a description of early theories concerning Tarot origins see S. Kaplan, *Tarot Classic*.
3 F. King, *Astral Projection, Magic and Alchemy*.
4 Ibid., pp.84-5.
5 R. Cavendish, *The Tarot*, p.146.
6 The Qlippoth are the 'negative' sephiroth which constitute the black Tree – the polar opposite of the transcendental shamanistic framework.
7 D. Miller, *The New Polytheism*, p.55.
8 Chakras are hypothetical energy centres in man, usually associated with the central nervous system.

Chapter 4: Surrealism and the Qabalah

1 A. Balakian, *Surrealism: The Road to the Absolute*, p.128.
2 J. Russell, *Max Ernst*, p.55.
3 J. H. Matthews, *An Introduction to Surrealism*, p.114.
4 Ibid., p.54.
5 Ibid., p.71.
6 M. Jean, *The History of Surrealist Painting*, p.207.
7 P. Waldo-Schwartz, *Art and the Occult*, p.102.
8 D. Sylvester, *Magritte*, p.14.
9 Included in L. Lippard (ed.), *Surrealists on Art*, p.155.
10 C. Castaneda, *The Teachings of Don Juan*, 1968, p.188.
11 Quoted in J. T. Soby, *Magritte*, p.7.
12 M. Jean, op.cit., p. 275.
13 J. T. Soby, *Yves Tanguy*, p.18.

14 See L. Lippard, op.cit., p.97.
15 While Laing's writings on the relativity of insanity are well known the extraordinary examination of hallucinatory insanity by Wilson Van Dusen is less so. Interested readers are referred to Van Dusen's *The Natural Depth in Man*, and his perceptive article 'Hallucinations as the World of Spirits' contained in John White's *Frontiers of Consciousness*.
16 P. Walton, *Dali/Miro*, p.7.
17 Quoted in G. Xuriguera, *Wilfredo Lam*, p.23.
18 Ibid., p.9.
19 Ibid., p.23.
20 N. Drury and S. Skinner, *The Search for Abraxas*, pp.49-71.
21 John Russell (1967: p.106) has written that Ernst's birds do not find themselves trapped in the forest and are invariably symbols of transcendence. The sun, mythologically, is the prime symbol of individuation – the spiritual focusing and harmonizing of the life processes.
22 Included in L. Lippard (ed.), op.cit., p.118 et seq.
23 Ibid., p.121.
24 A condensed account of Spare's sigil method is contained in N. Drury and S. Skinner, op.cit., Spare's major magical treatise *The Book of Pleasure*, which contains his most complete statement on sigils and magical energy, has recently been reissued (Montreal, 1976, 93 Publishing).
25 L. Lippard, op.cit., p.121.
26 M. Ernst, 'What is Surrealism?' in L. Lippard, op.cit., p.134.
27 J. Russell, op.cit., p.50.
28 J. Fadiman and R. Frager, *Personality and Personal Growth*, pp.306, 340.
29 J. Campbell, Introduction to M. Deren, *Divine Horsemen – Voodoo Gods of Haiti*, p.xiii.

Chapter 5: Magic and fantasy – the new visionary art

1 P. Max, *Superposter Book*.
2 P. Woodroffe, *Mythopoeikon*, p.2.
3 Ibid., p.10.
4 R. Masters and J. Houston, *Psychedelic Art*, p.82.
5 A. M. Klarwein, *Milk'n Honey*, (no numbered pages).
6 W. Hopps, *Visions*, p.vii.
7 R. Dean, *Views*, p.7.
8 J. Stellingwerff, *La Peinture Hermetique de Diana Vandenberg*, 1969, p.69.
9 Max Ernst's collage style has been a profound influence on Satty. Ernst similarly regarded himself as a visual alchemist and used this term to describe his first collage exhibition in Paris, May 1921.
10 W. Satty, *Time Zone*, p.II (Preface).
11 W. Satty, Ludlow's *The Hasheesh Eater*, 1975 – back cover note.
12 T. Albright, Introduction to W. Satty, *The Illustrated Edgar Allan Poe*, 1976.
13 W. Satty, *The Illustrated Edgar Allan Poe*, p.214.
14 W. Satty, *Time Zone*, p.II (Preface).

15 The 'assumption of the god form' in ceremonial magic is a practice whereby an occultist imitates the posture and manner of a mythological deity with the intention of embodying its essence through the act of identification.
16 Quoted in W. Glover's introduction to *The Art of Rosaleen Norton*, 1952.

Chapter 6: The rise of cosmic music

(Note: since many albums are released internationally, the following record references are by label and city of origin only.)

1 Country Joe and the Fish, *I Feel Like I'm Fixin to Die*, New York, Vanguard Records.
2 Steppenwolf, *Steppenwolf the Second*, New York, Dunhill Records.
3 The Incredible String Band, *Relics of the Incredible String Band*, London, Elektra Records.
4 The Incredible String Band, *Wild Horses*, London, Elektra Records.
5 Donovan, *Atlantis*, London, Epic Records.
6 The Rolling Stones, *Sympathy for the Devil*, London, Decca Records.
7 David Bowie, *Quicksand*, London RCA Records.
8 Graham Bond, *Holy Magick*, London, Vertigo Records.
9 Graham Bond, *We Put Our Magick On You*, London, Vertigo Records.
10 Judee Sill, *Judee Sill*, Los Angeles, Asylum Records.
11 The Band, *The Band*, New York, Capitol Records.
12 Pete Sinfield, *Still*, London, Manticore Records.
13 Various artists, *Woodstock*, New York, Atlantic Records.
14 Soundtrack, *2001*, New York, MGM Records.
15 Pink Floyd, *Ummagumma*, London, Harvest Records.
16 Ron Geesin and Roger Waters, *Music from the Body*, London, Harvest Records.
17 Pink Floyd, *Meddle*, London, Harvest Records.
18 Pink Floyd, *The Dark Side of the Moon*, London, Harvest Records.
19 Pink Floyd, *Wish You Were Here*, London, Harvest Records.
20 Hawkwind, *Space Ritual*, London, United Artists.
21 See *Yessongs, Relayers, Yesterday, Tales From Topographic Ocean*, London, Atlantic Records.
22 Steve Hackett, *Voyage of the Acolyte*, London, Charisma Records.
23 King Crimson, *Islands*, London, Island Records.
24 I. Macdonald, 'Head, Heart and Hips', and 'Fripp as the sexual athlete' – two interviews with Robert Fripp, *New Musical Express*, London, 25 August and 1 September 1973.
25 Robert Fripp and Brian Eno, *Evening Star*, London, Island Records.
26 Le Orme, *Felona and Serona*, London, Charisma Records.
27 Dzyan, *Time Machine*, Hamburg, Brain/Metronome.
28 Klaus Schulze, *Blackdance*, London, Virgin Records.
29 Klaus Schulze, *Cyborg*, Berlin, Ohr Records.
30 Yatha Sidra, *Meditation Mass*, Hamburg, Brain/Metronome.
31 Paul Horn, *Inside*, New York, Epic Records.
32 Walter Wegmuller, *Tarot*, Hamburg, Cosmic Couriers.

33 W. Y. Evans-Wentz, *The Fairy Faith in Celtic Countries*, New York, University Books Inc. 1966.
34 Bo Hansson, *Lord of the Rings*, London, Charisma Records.
35 Edgar Froese, *Aqua*, London, Virgin Records.

BIBLIOGRAPHY

References and recommended reading

Introduction: Counter-culture, magic and the new consciousness

Castaneda C., *The Teachings of Don Juan*, 1968, University of California Press; Harmondsworth, 1970, Penguin Books.

Castaneda, C., *A Separate Reality*, London, 1971, Bodley Head; Harmondsworth, 1973, Penguin Books.

Castaneda, C., *Journey to Ixtlan*, New York, 1974, Simon & Schuster; Harmondsworth, 1974, Penguin Books.

Castaneda C., *Tales of Power*, New York, 1972, Simon & Schuster.

Castaneda C., *A Second Ring of Power*, New York, 1978, Simon & Schuster.

Dean, R., *Views*, Surrey, 1975, Dragon's Dream.

De Mille, R., *Castaneda's Journey*, Santa Barbara, 1976, Capra Press.

Fry, P. and Long, M., *Beyond the Mechanical Mind*, Sydney, 1977, Australian Broadcasting Commission.

Grof, S., *Realms of the Human Unconscious*, New York, 1976, Dutton.

Hammond, D., *The Search for Psychic Power*, London, 1975, Hodder & Stoughton.

Harner, M. (ed.), *Hallucinogens and Shamanism*, New York, 1973, Oxford University Press.

Keen, S., *Voices and Visions*, New York, 1976, Harper & Row.

Krippner, S., *Song of the Siren*, New York, 1975, Harper & Row.

Larsen, S., *The Shaman's Doorway*, New York, 1976, Harper & Row.

Leary, T., *High Priest*, College Notes and Texts Inc., New York, 1968.

Leary, T., *The Psychedelic Experience*, New York, 1964, University Books Inc.

Lee P. R. *et al.*, *Symposium on Consciousness*, New York, 1977, Penguin Books.

Lilly, J., *Centre of the Cyclone*, London, 1973, Paladin.

Lilly, J., *Simulations of God*, New York, 1975, Simon & Schuster.

Masters, R. and Houston, J., *Mind Games*, London, 1973, Turnstone.

Monroe, R. *Journeys out of the Body*, New York, 1973, Doubleday.

Needleman, J., *A Sense of the Cosmos*, New York, 1976, Dutton.

Needleman, J., *The New Religions*, New York, 1970, Doubleday.

Ostrander, S. and Schroeder, L., *Psychic Discoveries Behind the Iron Curtain*, New York, 1971, Bantam Books.

Regardie, I., *Roll Away The Stone*, 1968, Saint Paul, Minn., Llewellyn.

Roszak, T., *The Making of a Counter-Culture*, London, 1970, Faber.

Roszak, T., *Unfinished Animal*, New York, 1975, Harper & Row.

Tart. C. (ed.), *Altered States of Consciousness*, New York, 1969, Wiley.

Bibliography

Tart. C. (ed.), *Transpersonal Psychologies*, London, 1975, Routledge & Kegan Paul.
Thompson, W. I., *Passages About Earth*, New York, 1973, Harper & Row.
Toffler, A., *Future Shock*, London, 1971, Pan Books.
Ullman, M. *et al.*, *Dream Telepathy*, London, 1973, Turnstone.
Weil, A., *The Natural Mind*, London, 1972, Jonathan Cape.
White, J. (ed.), *Frontiers of Consciousness*, New York, 1974, Avon.
White, J. (ed.), *The Highest States of Consciousness*, New York, 1972, Doubleday.

Chapter 1: The magical universe

Arieti, S., *Creativity: the Magical Synthesis*, New York, 1976, Basic Books Inc.
Bardon, F., *Initiation into Hermetics*, Koblenz, 1962, Osiris Verlag.
Bardon, F., *The Practice of Magical Evocation*, Graz, 1967, Rudolph Pravica.
Barrett, F., *The Magus*, New York, 1973, University Books/Citadel.
Chevalier, G., *The Sacred Magician*, London, 1976, Paladin.
Colquhoun, I., *Sword of Wisdom*, London, 1975, Neville Spearman.
Crowley, A., *Book 4*, Dallas, 1972, Sangreal Foundation.
Crowley, A., *Magick in Theory and Practice*, published privately in Paris, 1929.
Crowley, A., *The Qabalah of Aleister Crowley*, New York, 1973, Samuel Weiser.
Drury, N., *The Path of the Chameleon*, London, 1973, Neville Spearman.
Drury, N. and Skinner, S., *The Search for Abraxas*, London, 1972, Neville Spearman.
Halevi, Z. S., *Adam and the Kabbalistic Tree*, London, 1974, Rider.
Heenan, E. F., *Mystery, Magic and Miracle: Religion in a Post-Aquarian Age*, Englewood Cliffs, New Jersey, 1973, Prentice-Hall.
Howe, E., *The Magicians of the Golden Dawn*, London, 1972, Routledge & Kegan Paul.
Hughes, R. *Heaven and Hell in Western Art*, London, 1968, Weidenfeld & Nicolson.
King, F. (ed.), *Astral Projection, Magic and Alchemy*, London, 1973, Neville Spearman.
King, F. (ed.), *Ritual Magic in England*, London, 1970, Neville Spearman.
King, F. and Skinner, S., *Techniques of High Magic*, London, 1976, C. W. Daniel.
Mathers, S. L., *The Kabbalah Unveiled*, London, 1968, Routledge & Kegan Paul.
Mathers, S. L., *The Sacred Magic of Abramelin the Mage*, Chicago, 1948, De Laurence.
Pauwels, L. and Bergier, J., *The Dawn of Magic*, London, 1963, Anthony Gibbs and Phillips – subsequently retitled *The Morning of the Magicians*.
Regardie, I., *The Golden Dawn*, Vols 1-4, Chicago, 1937-40, Aries Press.
Regardie, I., *The Tree of Life*, London, 1932, Rider.
Schaya, L., *The Universal Meaning of the Kabbalah*, 1971, New Jersey, University Books Inc.
Scholem, G., *Kabbalah*, New York, 1975, Quadrangle/New York Times.
Spare, A. O. *The Book of Pleasure*, Montreal, 1976, 93 Publishing.
Waite, A. E., *The Brotherhood of the Rosy Cross*, New York, 1961, University Books Inc.

Bibliography

Waite, A. E., *The Holy Kabbalah*, New York, 1960, University Books Inc.
Waite, A. E., *The Pictorial Key to the Tarot*, New York, 1973, Samuel Weiser.
Wilson, C., *The Occult*, London, 1971, Hodder & Stoughton.
Zaretsky I. and Leone, M. (eds), *Religious Movements in Contemporary America*,
    1974, Princetown University Press.
Zimmer, H., *The King and the Corpse*, New York, 1960, Meridian.

Chapter 2: Archetypes and belief systems

Butler, W. E., *Magic, its Ritual Power and Purpose*, London, 1958, Aquarian
    Press.
Butler, W. E., *The Magician, his Training and Work*, London, 1959, Aquarian
    Press.
Edinger, E., *Ego and Archetype*, Baltimore, 1973, Penguin Books.
Eliade, M., *Cosmos and History*, New York, 1959, Harper & Row.
Eliade, M., *Shamanism*, London, 1952, Routledge & Kegan Paul.
Fortune, D., *Applied Magic*, London, 1962, Aquarian Press.
Fortune, D., *The Mystical Qabalah*, London, 1966, Ernest Benn.
Henderson, J., *Thresholds of Initiation*, Connecticut, 1967, Wesleyan University
    Press.
Jacobi, J., *The Psychology of C. G. Jung*, London, 1942, Routledge & Kegan Paul.
Jung, C. G., *The Archetypes of the Collective Unconscious*, London, 1959,
    Routledge & Kegan Paul.
Jung, C. G., *Aion*, London, 1959, Routledge & Kegan Paul.
Jung, C. G., *Man and his Symbols*, London, 1964, Aldus Books.
Jung. C. G., *Memories, Dreams and Reflections*, London, 1967, Fontana Books.
Jung. C. G., *Modern Man in Search of a Soul*, London, 1933, Routledge & Kegan
    Paul.
Jung. C. G., *The Integration of the Personality*, London, 1940, Kegan Paul,
    Trench, Trubner.
Jung. C. G., *The Structure and Dynamics of the Psyche*, London, 1959, Routledge
    & Kegan Paul.
Jung. C. G., *VII Sermones ad Mortuos*, London, 1967, Stuart & Watkins.
Lilly, J., *Centre of the Cyclone*, London, 1973, Paladin.
Lilly, J., *The Dyadic Cyclone*, New York, 1976, Simon & Schuster.
Lilly, J., *The Human Biocomputer*, London, 1974, Abacus.
Lilly, J., *Simulations of God*, New York, 1975, Simon & Schuster.
Regardie, I., *The Art and Meaning of Magic*, Cheltenham, 1964, Helios.
Roszak, T., *Unfinished Animal*, New York, 1975, Harper & Row.
Wolff, F. M., *Pathways Through to Space*, New York, 1973, Julian Press.

Chapter 3: The Tarot and transformation

Blakeley, J. D., *The Mystical Tower of the Tarot*, London, 1974, Robinson &
    Watkins.
Butler, B., *The Definitive Tarot*, London, 1975, Rider.
Butler, W. E., *Magic and the Qabalah*, London, 1964, Aquarian Press.

Case, P. F., *The Tarot*, New York, 1947, Macoy.

Cavendish, R., *The Tarot*, London, 1975, Michael Joseph.

Crowley, A., *The Book of Thoth*, New York, 1969, Samuel Weiser.

Drury, N., *Don Juan, Mescalito and Modern Magic*, London and Boston, 1977, Routledge & Kegan Paul.

Drury, N. (ed.), *Frontiers of Consciousness*, Melbourne, 1975, Greenhouse Press.

Drury, N., *The Path of the Chameleon*, London, 1973, Neville Spearman.

Eliade, M., *Shamanism*, London, 1952, Routledge & Kegan Paul.

Fortune, D., *The Mystical Qabalah*, 1966, London, Ernest Benn.

Gettings, F., *The Book of the Tarot*, London, 1973, Trewin Copplestone Publishing.

Gray, W. G., *The Ladder of Lights*, Cheltenham, 1968, Helios.

Hoeller, S. A., *The Royal Road*, Wheaton, Illinois, 1975, Quest Books.

Kaplan, S. R., *Tarot Classic*, New York, 1972, Grosset & Dunlap.

King, F. (ed.), *Astral Projection, Magic and Alchemy*, London, 1971, Neville Spearman.

Knight, G., *A Practical Guide to Qabalistic Symbolism*, Vols 1 and 2, Cheltenham, 1965, Helios.

Lévi, E., *The History of Magic*, London, 1913, Rider.

Miller, D., *The New Polytheism*, New York, 1974, Harper & Row.

Ouspensky, P. D., *The Symbolism of the Tarot*, New York, 1976, Dover.

Regardie, I., *The Golden Dawn*, Vols 1-4, Chicago, 1937-40, Aries Press.

Waite, A. E., *The Pictorial Key to the Tarot*, New York, 1963, Samuel Weiser.

Waite, A. E., *The Mysteries of Magic*, New Jersey, 1974, University Books Inc.

Zimmer, H., *The King and the Corpse*, New York, 1960, Meridian.

Chapter 5: Magic and fantasy – the new visionary art

Balakian, A., *Surrealism: The Road to the Absolute*, London, 1973, Allen and Unwin.

Barreda, C., *Paalen*, Mexico City, 1967, Museum of Modern Art.

Cardinal, R. and Short, R. S., *Surrealism: Permanent Revolution*, London, 1970, Studio Vista.

Castaneda, C., *The Teachings of Don Juan*, 1968, University of California Press; Harmondsworth, 1970, Penguin Books.

Deren, M., *Divine Horsemen – Voodoo Gods of Haiti*, London, 1970, Thames & Hudson.

Diehl, G., *Max Ernst*, New York, 1973, Crown.

Drury, N. and Skinner, S., *The Search for Abraxas*, London, 1972, Neville Spearman.

Ernst, M., *Maximiliana*, Munich, 1975, Bruckmann.

Fadiman, J. and Frager, R., *Personality and Personal Growth*, New York, 1976, Harper & Row.

Grant, K., *Images and Oracles of Austin Osman Spare*, London, 1975, Muller.

Jean, M., *The History of Surrealist Painting*, London, 1960, Weidenfeld & Nicolson.

Larkin, D. (ed.), *Dali*, London, 1974, Pan Books.

Lévy, J., *Surrealism*, New York, 1968, Arno.

Lippard, L. (ed.), *Surrealists on Art*, Englewood Cliffs, New Jersey, 1970, Prentice-Hall.

Matthews, J. H., *An Introduction to Surrealism*, 1965, Pennsylvania State University Press.

Russell, J., *Max Ernst*, London, 1967, Thames & Hudson.

Sandrow, N., *Surrealism, Theatre and Ideas*, New York, 1972, Harper & Row.

Soby, J. T., *Magritte*, New York, 1965, Museum of Modern Art.

Soby, J. T., *Yves Tanguy*, New York, 1955, Museum of Modern Art.

Spies, W., *Max Ernst 1950-70*, New York, 1971, Abrams.

Sylvester, D., *Magritte*, London, 1969, Arts Council of Great Britain.

Terrasse, A., *Paul Delvaux*, Chicago, 1973, J. Philip O'Hara Inc.

Van Dusen, W. *The Natural Depth in Man*, New York, 1972, Harper & Row.

Waldberg, P., *Surrealism*, London, 1965, Thames & Hudson.

Waldo-Schwarz, P., *Art and the Occult*, New York, 1975, Braziller.

Walton, P., *Dali/Miro*, New York, 1967, Tudor.

White, J. (ed.), *Frontiers of Consciousness*, New York, 1975, Avon.

Xuriguera, G., *Wilfredo Lam*, Paris, 1974, Filipacchi.

Chapter 5: Magic and fantasy – the new visionary art

Arguelles, J. and M., *Mandala*, Berkeley, California, 1972, Shambala.

Ballantine, B., *The Fantastic World of Gervasio Gallardo*, New York, 1976, Peacock/Bantam.

Dean, R., *Views*, Surrey, 1975, Dragon's Dream.

Gettings, F., *Arthur Rackham*, London, 1975, Studio Vista.

Giger, H. R., *Necronomicon*, London, 1978, Big O Publishing.

Hopps, W., *Visions*, Corte Madera, California, 1976, Pomegranate Publications.

Klarwein, A. M., *God Jokes*, New York, 1976, Harmony. *Milk'n Honey*, New York, 1973, Harmony.

Larkin, D. (ed.), *The Fantastic Kingdom*, New York, 1974, Ballantine.

Masters, R. and Houston, J., *Psychedelic Art*, London, 1968, Weidenfeld & Nicolson.

Max, P., *Superposter Book*, New York, 1971, Crown.

Mrazek, W., *Ars Phantastica*, Vienna, 1970, IM Eigenverlag.

Norton, R., *The Art of Rosaleen Norton*, Sydney, 1952, Walter Glover.

Peppin, B., *Fantasy*, London, 1975, Studio Vista.

Satty, W., *The Illustrated Edgar Allan Poe*, New York, 1976, Clarkson N. Potter Inc.

Satty, W., Ludlow's *The Hasheesh Eater*, San Francisco, Level Press, 1975.

Satty, W., *Time Zone*, San Francisco, 1973, Straight Arrow.

Satty, W., *The Cosmic Bicycle*, San Francisco, 1971, Straight Arrow.

Stellingwerff, J., *La Peinture Hermetique de Diana Vandenberg*, Amsterdam, 1969, Buijten and Schipperheijn.

Watney, S., *Fantastic Painters*, London, 1977, Thames & Hudson.

Woodroffe, P., *Mythopoeikon*, Surrey, 1976, Dragon's World.

Chapter 6: The rise of cosmic music

Drury, N., 'Cosmic Textures – Klaus Schulze, Ash Ra Tempel, Dzyan, Annexus Quam . . .', Sydney, June 1975, *Cosmos*, Vol.2, No.II.

Drury, N., 'Magic, Mysticism and Pop Music' in N. Drury (ed.), *Frontiers of Consciousness*, Melbourne, 1975, Greenhouse Press.

Drury, N., 'New Pathways – Progressive Rock and the Music of Inner Space', Sydney, August 1974, *Cosmos*, Vol.2, No.1.

Drury, N., 'The Implications of Magic in the Creative Process', Sydney, 1976, *New Poetry*, Vol.24, No.2.

Drury, N., 'The Music of Texture', Sydney, November 1974, *Cosmos*, Vol.2, No.4.

Drury, N., 'The Inner Space Movement', Sydney, 23 September 1976, *Rolling Stone* (Australian Edition), No.222.

Evans-Wentz, W. Y., *The Fairy Faith in Celtic Countries*, New York, 1966, University Books Inc.

Macdonald, I., 'Head Heart and Hips', London, 25 August 1973, *New Musical Express*.

Macdonald, I., 'Fripp as the Sexual Athlete', London, 1 September 1973, *New Musical Express*.

~ Index ~

Index

Waite, A. E., 7, 19, 51, 111, 119
Waters, R., 117, 118
Wegmuller, W., 123
Weil, A., 2
Westcott, W., 20
Wilson, C., 14

Woodroffe, P., 90-1
Wright, D., 90

Yeats, W. B., 20, 21, 107, 112

Zimmer, H., 25